LIFE SKILLS FOR TEENS

A Practical & Essential Handbook to Independence

KIMBERLY P. MADDEN

Contents

Intro: You've Got This!

You made it to your teens! Welcome to this wonderful chapter of your life.

This is an exciting and dynamic time! You might be wondering how adults do some of the things they do. Or you might want to get out and figure things out on your own. Either way, your interest in gaining independence is right on time!

In these years, you'll prepare for freedom! Woot!

There are many skills to master, and luckily you don't need to know everything all at once. This book is a reference to guide and support you through life skills you'll benefit from in your teen years. These include basic cooking, nutrition, cleaning and clothing care, home maintenance skills, transportation, and personal safety.

In addition, essential life skills include money management, doing the right things to land a great job, and staying safe online and off.

Life skills also include less tangible yet foundational concepts like feeling successful, cultivating healthy relationships, managing tricky emotions, and designing a happy, fulfilling life.

It may seem like a lot, but this is just another starting point. And your *journey* is the key. Learning the skills themselves will support your voyage to independence, yes. And there are noble qualities, and characteristics gained while striving *toward* your life of greater freedom.

You'll learn new ways of thinking, how to analyze your options, and develop problem-solving abilities. You'll naturally develop more self-awareness, recognize your impact on others, and take responsibility for your actions. You'll build self-confidence and feel successful as you accomplish more. You'll build agility and be able to manage adversity in a healthy way.

In short, **you'll be a happier and more well-rounded individual.** There's nothing to lose.

Remember to be patient with yourself as you embark on new territory. Being independent is a process that takes time and includes trials, tribulations, triumphs, and transitions. Not to mention the physiological changes happening to your body during this phase that contribute to some of the mental, emotional, and social fog you might feel.

This is perfectly normal, and I promise you'll get through it.

Everyone who picks up this book will be at a different learning place. You might be on the younger side of your teens and have never cooked anything for yourself. Maybe you're a little older and know how to make meals and clean up, but you've never had to manage money and want to buy a car.

Or you may be in the older part of your teens where you're already reasonably independent, ready to live alone but may need some emotional support.

No matter where you're at during these precious teen years, you'll take steps toward being self-reliant and owning your independence with this book as a resource.

I promise, by reading this book, you'll feel served. And if you're the loving parent who invested in this book for your teen, well done. I assure you this book is valuable, and you're supporting your young Star to be more self-sufficient.

This book is organized into easy-to-read chapters, with clear steps and illustrations. You can still ask Mr. Google for help or check with Miss YouTube. And, of course, you have your friends and family to lean on too. This book is a clear and straightforward resource so you can get answers quickly, on your own.

This collection of critical life skills will prepare you to be more independent and feel successful, starting now!

I wholeheartedly believe all teens can (and do) learn to be self-reliant. This happens at all sorts of levels based on different upbringings and backgrounds. For teens with special needs or special circumstances, some life skills may be harder to master due to differences in cognitive development. With patience, preparation, and perseverance, any teen can learn life skills. This book, however, has been written for the able-bodied teen.

Although I can't promise you an adolescence devoid of struggle, I aim to help you build **competence, capability,** and **confidence** so you can love yourself, love others, and love life!

Let's begin the journey into adulthood and beyond!

ONE

Show Me The MONEY!

Let's get to some good stuff right away! Money! You've likely already had experiences or interactions with money in your life. It could be getting an allowance, asking your folks to pay for new shoes, or using your saved-up cash to buy something at the store.

Here's the deal. You've *gotta* learn all about money to gain independence from mom and dad. And for whatever reason, most traditional public schools won't teach this to you.

I'll be honest, though. Your financial future rides on a lot of factors, for example, where you were brought up or the amount of wealth within your family. But when you start young, educate yourself about money, finances, and how these play out, you'll significantly (and positively) affect your financial future.

So read on... because soon - you'll be in control of your money and be making decisions that will influence your bank account.

OK, so what IS Money?

Money is a medium of exchange. We use it to trade for goods and services, and it's always been around. Even waaaay before *money*, items were traded for value.

Money is used in many different currencies around the World to live. You've probably heard the phrase 'Money makes the World go Round.' Well, it's true. So it's essential to understand the value of money and how it works.

There are lots of ways money is used: buying physical items like clothing or that new phone you have. You can pay for services, like a haircut, and money is used to pay for the place you live, either in rent or mortgage payments. You can even buy something that costs a lot and is paid over time, like a vehicle. (Payments are made each month toward the balance owed.)

You can place your money in certain places you believe will GROW. This is called Investing, and you leave your money in accounts that *hopefully* increase in value over time.

Having access to money also offers opportunities to share kindness and be generous. You could donate to charitable organizations, pitch in gas money to a buddy, buy a special gift for someone you care about, or buy a meal for the man that lives on the corner.

There are endless ways to use this valuable resource called money.

Certainly, it feels fantastic to have lots of money. However, it can be lost easily also, so money should be respected. Having money and using it wisely offers great freedom.

When money is managed correctly, backed with knowledge around how we earn it, save it, and make it grow, this creates positive leaps for life *later*. The payoff is ahead.

Yep, I know... that might be a hard pill to swallow. However, it's super helpful to get a grip on money NOW (while your responsibilities are still relatively few). You'll be better off in years to come. Trust me, your 'Future You' will be grateful.

What's Interest?

Well, there's good news & bad news. You can buy something that costs a lot and get it immediately by setting up monthly installments until the balance is paid off.

However, it's easy to be fooled in Finance Land. When you obtain something NOW that you continue to pay for LATER, you often pay additional service charges.

Let me break it down into easy numbers to illustrate. If you agree to buy something that costs $1200, let's say, and it's paid over a year. You would think - I'll pay $100 a month for 12 months, right?

Unfortunately, wrong. A *percentage of interest* is added each month, and you end up paying more than $100 per month. Yikes! (The exact rate will vary and is agreed upon before buying the item.)

More good news now. When your money is saved somewhere, like in a bank account or investment options, you actually EARN interest at a certain percentage. Let's say you have a bank account and put $1000 in now. The bank account has an interest rate of 0.03%, which is $30 per year. And while that's not a lot of extra money, you did absolutely nothing for it!

The key to understanding how interest works is this: If you want to borrow money, you usually have to pay for it. But if you make deposits into an account, you can earn money, too.

Now that you've got the basics let's get into how you can track what you're saving and spending.

Budgeting Money

Budgeting has two sides - what you're spending and what you're saving. To save more, you have to spend less. That's the simplest way to put it.

Buying something looks as easy as tapping a plastic card. It's not surprising to think there's an endless number of times you can tap. But unfortunately, it's not so!

By keeping track of your own funds in an account and then seeing the amount change with each purchase, you'll quickly understand the value of each dollar. This is essential budgeting basics.

There are a few good ways to do this. You can track spending by writing down your purchases in a notebook you carry with you. You could ask for receipts for everything and then manually add them to a spreadsheet. You can also add many apps to your phone to make tracking super easy.

Track spending and be aware of account balances. See what's left over in the bank accounts at the end of the day, week or month after you've spent. And try to *spend less*. Spending is the easy part, trust me! Practice saying 'no thanks' to that new sweater you want and make your own lunch instead of buying out. If you have a hard time saying no, try leaving cash and cards at home to remove the temptation.

This will surely create a little money manager out of you and is such an important skill to master.

Let's talk about the other side of budgeting, which is saving. Start by ensuring you have at least one savings account in the bank where you can put your money. If you're under 18, you'll likely need a parent to help set this up. Typically, you spend from your Checking account, and you can save in your Savings accounts.

And then, when money comes IN (from gifts, a part-time job, an allowance, etc.), *get into the habit* of dividing it into percentages. I've outlined an example of what percentages could look like. When it comes to budgeting, you should do what works best for you, so feel free to update these as you see fit.

<u>Basic Living Expenses - 55%</u>

This will vary from person to person and depend on what stage you're in. But these expenses include rent, utilities, transportation, food, etc. The necessities. It's a good idea to start at 55%, even though you may only need some of this right away. Extra can always be saved up for later as things shift. Remember, at some point, you will be moving out (if you haven't already). And bills tend to add up. So if you have a surplus in this account, you'll be better off later.

<u>Education - 10%</u>

You got it. Start thinking about your educational future early. This could be for post-secondary school tuition, a hands-on course to gain knowledge, books, mentoring, etc. Start putting 10% of your money aside here.

<u>Long-Term Savings - 10%</u>

Put this money away, and don't touch it. It's not meant for a rainy day. It's intended for your future, like your retirement (Woah!). Put 10% of your money in and forget about it.

Short-Term Savings - 10%

This should go toward larger purchases you need to save up for. It could include that new gaming system you want, a nice handbag, a grad trip, or even a vehicle! You can save for more than one thing. For example, you could put 5% toward the trip and 5% toward a car.

Fun - 10%

Put some of your money toward good times and things you enjoy! This is for music, books, movies, etc. Use this money to head to the fair, get your hair or nails done, or go to a play. Enjoy spending on yourself! You don't HAVE to spend all of this. It's just important to have some funds for enjoyment.

Giving - 5%

I recommend at least a 5% account which you use to buy gifts for others or for charitable donations. This account could definitely go up during holiday time!

Keep in mind the HABIT is more important than the amounts you're contributing. Even if you're not earning much yet. Or the only money you have is when grandma gives you a holiday gift. Perfect! This process will help you become financially responsible and support a massive milestone to independence.

If you're not earning regular income yet, here are some ideas to help you get going.

- Make an arrangement with mom and dad to do some housework or extra chores
- Get a summer job
- Petsit / Babysit

- Have a Garage Sale (of your belongings or those agreed on with mom and dad, please!)
- Create something to sell on Etsy
- List some items you're ready to part with on an online board like Craigslist or Facebook Marketplace
- Sell a service like mowing/raking lawns, car washing, or shoveling driveways

And just as important, remember where you can take advantage of savings. Often, using your student ID will get you great deals. Remember to ask about student discounts when you go places. And coupons often show up in the mail and are everywhere online, so take advantage of those too. Getting deals can make saving easier and lets you put away more of what you earn.

Understanding Credit & Debt

Credit & debt are related. Debt refers to the total amount of borrowed money (in loans, credit cards, etc.). Credit is the *ability to borrow* money with the expectation you'll repay.

Debt is how much you owe today. And credit is how much you can borrow in the future.

How you pay off the debt contributes to your credit health, which is graded as a score. So if you pay on time, great! You're building good credit. But if you continually miss payments, your score is negatively affected.

Good credit gives you access to an item before it's paid off. But generally, a credit arrangement isn't free and includes monthly service charges. Remember to weigh out your options when considering buying something on credit. While it may seem exciting to own something expensive right away instead of saving up for it, your credit score is impacted if payments are missed.

Giving Back

It's never too early to begin giving back. And any amount is worth it. Regularly giving your money to something you believe in or those in need builds empathy, appreciation, and gratitude. Earlier, I recommended 5% of whatever income you have coming in be set aside for Giving.

This 5% includes doing nice things for people you know. But I also want to stress the importance of giving back to people you *don't* know.

Being fortunate and having money is a beautiful gift. Consider offering some of our fortunes to others who have fewer opportunities. It doesn't have to be a lot. Try half of your 'Giving' account (2.5%).

Choose an organization that supports something you're passionate about. For example, donate to your local SPCA or animal shelter if you love animals. If you feel passionate about kids, how about World Vision or The Children's Foundation.

In addition to money, please consider donating time and volunteering locally. This is very impactful as well.

Wrapping it Up

To master money, you need to manage money, and this is the key to financial freedom. Remember the A-B-C's of Good Finances, and you'll be well on your way!

A - Account Management. Monitor your accounts and know where your money is.

B - Budgeting. Track your spending, plan ahead for large purchases and save as much as possible.

C - Credit. This is different from cash and costs more in the long term. Ensure timely repayment to avoid more fees and a negative mark on your credit score.

We all come from different circumstances and backgrounds, so each of us will have a different experience with money. Managing your money will set you up for inevitable success and independence. And if you can get started NOW - you'll rock this.

Kim's Corner: *Can Money Buy Happiness??*

I imagine you've heard the saying before. Most people would say, 'No Way! Happiness comes from within…." True. And…

Money IS important to happiness. Ask anyone who doesn't have it. Having more money can offer access to homes in safer areas, better health care, better nutrition, and more free time to enjoy life.

But at some point, the effects of having lots of money decreases. Turns out - DOING makes us happier than HAVING. Even though it might seem exciting to have the latest and greatest new phone or shoes, these items eventually fade into the background and become the new normal.

But you can use your money to gain valuable experiences with others, create memories and stories to tell people, and of course, give to others.

When money is managed with care to experience life and support others less fortunate, you will enjoy more long-term happiness.

TWO

Kitchen Skillz

L et's get cooking, shall we? The kitchen is often the place with the most hustle and bustle. Whether making your own food with a few friends or at a party, the kitchen is often where all the buzz is. But you may not have much experience there yet.

You might have walked past it several times or joined mom or dad while cooking dinner. Here's the deal. Part of being independent is knowing your way around the kitchen and learning how to prepare and grocery shop for your own meals. This way, you know exactly what you're eating, which is best for your health (and it costs less!). Let's sort out some Kitchen Mysteries you might be wondering about.

Meet ... The Kitchen!

First, get to know what's in your kitchen because every kitchen is different. But all will have essential appliances and utensils. Let's quickly breeze through them, so you have an idea of what these items are.

Appliances

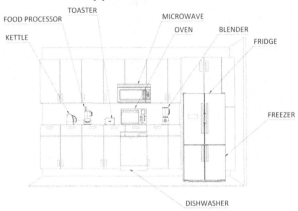

Cookware, Tableware & Cutlery

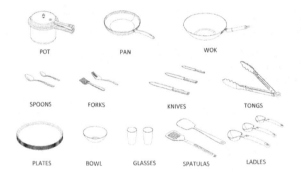

The appliances in your specific kitchen may vary depending on where you are in the World. In Britain, for instance, the washing machine can be found in the kitchen. And in European kitchens, some of these small appliances are not generally used. Wherever you live, the most important is having a good, working knowledge of the basic kitchen items used daily.

Set the Table

In the fast-paced Gen-Z land, setting the table has become less important. But the formality is not lost!

If you're wondering why on earth you should set the table, I've listed some reasons.

- When you set the table, you set the proper atmosphere (there are definitely social protocols for interacting at the table).
- It makes your food look better.
- It's a great way to gain points with mom and dad and be helpful!
- When guests join you at the table, it shows they're welcome.

Every culture has its own protocol for setting the table, but we'll focus on the steps for two main ones; the everyday-dinner setting and the formal setting.

Informal Dinner Setting

The everyday dinner table setting is pretty straightforward and can be done in six steps:

Informal Setting

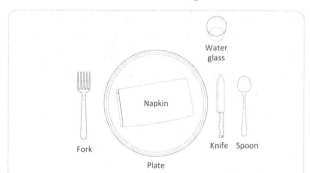

1. Lay your table with a place mat if you decide to use one.

2. Put your dinner plate in the middle of the placemat.

3. Place the napkin on top of the dinner plate. (It can also be folded under the fork.)

4. The fork should be placed on the left side of the dinner plate.

5. The knife should be on the right side, with the salad knife next to that.

6. The spoon is placed to the right of the knife if needed.

7. Lastly, set the water glass to be slightly above the knife on the right side.

Formal Table Setting

Use this setting when you want to impress someone special or when hosting a dinner party. Setting the table for a formal event can be initially daunting. With practice, you'll eventually get the hang of it.

Formal Setting

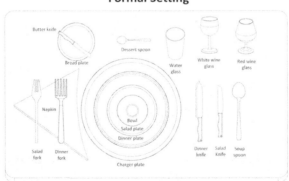

1. Place a neatly ironed tablecloth on the table.

2. Place the largest plate (charger) on the table and put the dinner plate on it.

3. Place the salad plate on the dinner plate and the soup bowl on the salad plate if there's soup.

4. Put the dinner fork on the left side of the dinner plate and a salad fork to the left of the dinner fork.

5. Place the napkin on the dinner plate, or under the forks. You can also use napkin rings.

6. The dinner knife should be on the right side of the dinner plate, and the soup spoon to the right side of the dinner knife. Note that the blade of the dinner knife should face inwards.

7. Place the bread plate towards the top left side of the charger plate. You could also have the butter knife placed horizontally on the bread plate, with the blade facing downward.

8. At the top of the charger plate, place the dessert spoon with its handle pointing towards the right.

9. There should be three glasses on the table, and they all go to the top right side of the charger plate; the water, white wine, and red wine glasses. Place the water glass closest to the charger plate, just above the dinner knife. The red wine glass should be farthest from the charger plate, and the white wine glass should be somewhere between.

Now that you can set the table, let's get to what you can make.

Meal Planning

Meal Planning is as simple as it sounds - you plan what to eat. A meal plan can be as comprehensive as a four-week outline, while another can just lay out meals for a week. Any way you do this, you'll benefit when planning ahead and making your own food.

- It costs you less for groceries when you're super organized about what you're eating.
- You won't have to stress about what to make at every meal (no decision fatigue!).

- It'll help you reach your health goals faster.
- You waste less food.

If you've just moved out, you might think, 'Woot! I can eat whatever I want now!' But let me tell you that being in charge of your health is a great responsibility. View your body as a temple and treat it with respect. Feed it with wholesome, nourishing, healthy foods, and you will always be physically at your best.

When planning your meals, remember to get all or most of the food groups (grains, proteins, fruits & vegetables, and low-fat dairy) in each meal. Eating healthy helps you grow well and strong.

What matters most is that whatever meals you plan out, stick with them!

Whether you're active in sports, dance, drama, music, math clubs, and so on, or you're not as busy right now, you need food **ENERGY**!

Be conscious of *what* you eat and *when* you eat. And remember to drink lots of water. Having a plan makes this easier.

To make meal planning a success, prepare some meals and/or ingredients ahead of time. For instance, take some time on the weekend to chop all the veggies you'll eat during the week. Or you can batch-cook rice or potatoes and keep them refrigerated, which saves time during busy weekdays.

See the following Sample Meal Plan for ideas. Hopefully, it inspires you!

Day	Breakfast	Lunch	Dinner	Snack
1	2 slices whole wheat toast with 2 tbsp Peanut butter 1 cup yogurt	Tuna pasta	Grilled chicken breasts with roasted veggies	Handful of Nuts, Apple
2	1 cup Oatmeal with coconut milk and blueberries	Turkey sandwich 1 cup orange juice	Small steak with roasted sweet potatoes	Banana
3	2 Scrambled eggs Almond milk	1 cup Brown rice Sauteed veggies	Turkey with mashed potato and corn	Wheat crackers 1 cup fresh raspberries
4	Whole wheat English muffin with low-fat cheese	Pasta + tomato sauce	Grilled chicken and garden salad	Handful of cashews
5	Pancakes and berries	1 cup ground pork fried rice with green peppers	Vegetable stirfry with noodles	1 cup of low-fat yogurt
6	Green smoothie	Grilled salmon with large garden salad	Chicken burger and salad	1 cup baby carrots
7	Egg muffins with sausage	Oven grilled cheese	1 cup white rice with beef stirfry	1 cup popcorn with small amount of salt

Simple Recipes

Recipes are countless! The number of recipes available online and in cookbooks can be overwhelming.

Recipe ideas are also all over the backs of food packages. If you're looking for inspiration, you'll find it everywhere!

Below are some basic but important staple foods to know how to make.

Hard / Soft Boil an Egg

Gently add your eggs to a pot (don't crowd) and cover it with at least an inch of water. Bring your water to a rolling boil, turn off the heat, and cover it with a lid. Depending on how you like your eggs, you can leave them in for longer (4 - 12 mins). You can always sacrifice one of the eggs to see if it's ready the way you like it! Run the egg under cold water and peel the shell off to cut it open.

Pasta Noodles

Fill your pot up with water and bring it to a boil. Put your noodles in, and ensure they are covered by water. Add a pinch of salt. Cook for roughly 8 - 10 min, depending on the type of pasta. Stir occasionally to prevent clumping. Check to see if the pasta is ready by trying one. And then drain!

Hot Dog

Boil some water on the stove, add in your hot dog and wait! Give it about 7 mins, and you're good to go!

Rice / Quinoa

Generally, most rice and quinoa are water to grain 2:1. This means 2 cups of water to 1 cup of dry food. But read the label before starting, as this is just a guideline. Boil your water first and add any spice or butter required in the recipe from the package. Turn the heat right down and add your grain. Simmer with the lid on for the time noted on the box, usually from 20 to 45 minutes.

Cooking is a significant life skill and can be fun if you really take it on. Often teens will shy away from cooking for fear of messing it up. But don't fear! As with any other skill, the more you practice, the better you'll get. Truth is, even the best chefs in the world mess up their meals once in a while. Start with the basics and expand from there.

Store The Extras

Yay leftovers! Pasta, soups, rice… you name it. Some foods are left-over-worthy! But the question is, how do you store them safely?

Storing food the right way is fundamental. Let's look at ways to keep your leftovers safe from going bad and making you sick.

Food can be grouped into 3 types for storage purposes: perishable, semi-perishable, and non-perishable. This means some foods do well on the countertop, some belong in the refrigerator, and some require freezing to last.

Perishable foods can't be stored for long periods at room temperature. They need to be kept either in the fridge or freezer. These foods include eggs, meats, seafood, poultry, raw fruits, peppers, and vegetables. Cooked foods are also perishable. For already cooked leftovers, don't wait more than 2 hours before throwing them into the fridge.

Semi-perishable foods don't require immediate refrigeration but will spoil more quickly than non-perishable items. There are foods like dried fruits, flour, bread, cereal, potatoes, onions, etc. For instance, potatoes, flour, and grains do well in dry, well-ventilated spaces and stay in good condition for months. While bread should be tossed into the freezer if you want it to last longer.

Non-perishable foods can be stored for a long time without going bad and have a long shelf life. These include dried beans, canned foods, grains, rice, teabags, coffee, nut butter, and much more. These don't necessarily require refrigeration, although after you open something canned, you'd want to pop it in the fridge (like nut butter).

Remember to handle food properly. Wash your hands well, keep your kitchen counter and surface areas clean, cook foods properly, and separate raw foods from those all set for munching.

Please be especially careful with raw chicken to avoid salmonella poisoning. Having a separate cutting board for raw meat is best, ensuring that nothing touches your clean plates or bowls. When you're done, spray them with a well-diluted bleach mixture to kill off bacteria. Wash your cutting board and utensils used for the raw meat in hot, soapy water.

Finally, check the 'best before' and the expiration date. If you suspect food has gone bad, just toss it, k? There is no point in tasting something that could make you sick.

Grocery Shopping

When you *finally* gain the independence you really want, you may learn that buying food takes a large chunk of your money. (Time to give mum and dad a THANK YOU!)

When grocery shopping, there are things you can do to minimize cost.

- Avoid grocery shopping when you're hungry. This is an epic fail because the brain only signals FOOD, FOOD, and more FOOD. To reduce the temptation to buy every tasty snack item on the store shelves, have a nutritious meal at home before heading out.
- Have a list before heading out and determine to stick with it. This keeps you grounded and focused. Keep a working list somewhere handy, like on your fridge, and add to it when you think of something.
- Go shopping once a week only. This is wise because multiple visits to the store can cause you to spend more. Grab everything in one organized trip.
- Compare prices. There is nothing wrong with trying something cheaper. Some store brands may be just as good as premium brands. Give them a try.
- Buy foods in bulk and store them properly. You can also cook in bulk and keep some items in the freezer, making for easy meals later.
- Don't fall for the "on-sale" gimmick. It only makes sense if the item on sale is already on your list and you actually need it.
- Be organized. Keep your kitchen and pantry cupboards organized to easily see what you have. Then add what you don't have to your shopping list.

You can do this! Remember, everything takes practice, and soon, you'll be a grocery store pro!

Kim's Corner: *How you FEEL about your body matters!*

The relationship you cultivate with food is so important. It can be hard to care about our bodies the right way due to unhealthy images and messages on social media, TV, movies, magazines, and its focus on *how* we look.

In reality, behind every screen and inside every home, everyone has to work at loving, accepting, and honoring themselves and their bodies.

Remember, you are loved, whole, and perfect. No matter what size you are!

Do guys have body image issues?

Absolutely! Having a negative body image is an 'everyone' challenge. But the WAY it can affect us can be different. For example, guys are more likely to want big muscles and will lift weights and/or take steroids (big risks here, guys!) or supplements. Gals are more likely to try to attain 'thin-ness' and augment their feminine features.

Of course, there are exceptions here. Boys can also have eating disorders to try and be thinner, while girls can aspire to be stronger. These are just examples of how guys and gals may be affected differently by body issues.

I'm considered large, but I exercise and eat right! What's up with that?

Healthy bodies come in all sizes! Some bodies are naturally larger, and it's OK! Eating well will ensure your body gets what it needs to feel good. And regular movement will also help you maintain your health. A lot is coming into play here: your genes, culture, and hormone levels, to name a few.

Sometimes peoples' bodies stay a particular size because it's the size they *should* be at. Nothing wrong here! I know there's a lot of pressure to change our bodies. And this pressure can cause us to do unhealthy things like eat too little, exercise too intensely, or try those risky steroids… just don't do that!

To sum this up, you deserve to feel good about your body, whatever size you are! Nobody has the right to tell you to change your body, not family or friends or anyone. You can be healthy, happy, fit, and beautiful no matter your body size. Just keep eating well and exercising to stay healthy.

THREE

Keepin' It Clean! (Personal Grooming)

Hygiene is super duper important. You may feel like it doesn't matter if you skip a shower or don't brush your teeth, but I assure you, it definitely matters! Proper hygiene isn't just about cleaning to impress someone. It's what's healthiest for you, too!

Why Keep Clean?

The number one reason you should keep your body clean is to avoid getting sick and exposing yourself to unnecessary infections and diseases. This may seem extreme (and kinda gross), but things like tooth decay, lice, scabies, diarrhea, and worms, can be prevented with proper and regular hygiene practices.

Keeping clean is also a social responsibility. You wouldn't want someone to *smell* you before they *saw* you, right?? When you take proper care of your body, you can freely and confidently interact socially.

In addition, your body is going through a lot of changes. For example, many hormonal shifts are happening, and hair growth in new parts of your body could show up. Your body may start to have a different smell. And this can absolutely be managed with proper hygiene.

Keeping clean helps to develop discipline. It takes effort to get up in the morning, shower, brush your teeth, take care of yourself, and so on. Begin building a disciplined self-care practice now, and you'll benefit from this for years to come!

Changes, Changes, Changes!

OK, you've heard it before - puberty. It happens to both girls and boys, and it starts at different times and lasts for various lengths of time. Girls typically begin anywhere from ages 8 - 13, and boys can start anywhere from 10 - 14 years old. We're all unique, so this is just a general trend.

A lot is going on here. And it's NOT just physical (although this is a major part of puberty). You'll experience emotional changes and feel differently as your brain sends messages to your body through hormones.

Puberty is similar - but different for girls and boys. Some changes occur to both, like the appearance of pubic and underarm hair, a new body odor, and those dreaded pimples. And some changes will be different, like ejaculation and menstrual periods. Boys will see hair appear on their faces and notice their voices changing. Girls notice their breasts coming in and possibly stronger emotional shifts.

This is all a normal stage of life, and we've all gotta go through it on some level. There are physical as well as emotional changes. Still, the gist of puberty is that your body is *capable* of making a baby. (This doesn't necessarily mean you *should*, k?...)

If you engage in sexual activity, please understand that getting pregnant is a very real risk, and safe and responsible sexual precautions should be taken.

Personal Practices

- **Daily Shower or Bath:** Body odor is quite common at this phase because you develop new sweat glands in your armpits and private parts. This is even more critical for teens that engage in physical activities like sports. Remember to put on deodorant after your shower each morning and have a quick rinse after a good sweat from a game or workout.
- **Wash Hair Regularly:** Your hair gets dirty. Yes, it actually does. Certain hormones can also cause your hair to be oily and smelly. Unless your hair is dirty (like after sweating), you don't necessarily have to *shampoo* your hair every day. For some hair types, this can actually dry out and damage hair. Your hair is all different, but generally, be sure to wash your hair every other day using mild shampoo.
- **Skin Care:** Skin care is important. A lot of skin infections are caused because of poor hygiene. Besides, as you get into your teenage years, you may notice your skin starts getting oilier than usual. Oily skin gives an avenue for dirt to be trapped. Add face washing to your daily routine, and wear sunscreen to protect your skin from harsh UV rays.
- **Brush Hair and Get Haircuts:** Always brush your hair. The longer it is, the greater the need to style it. When your hair gets long, some kinds of hair types can get split ends, which means the hair splits at the end! It creates a frizzy look, and a haircut keeps your hair healthy and will help it grow and stay strong!
- **Brush and Floss:** Brushing your teeth twice daily helps remove icky bacteria that cause bad breath and prevents disease. At the end of the day, floss to remove any food left between your teeth.
- **Shave Regularly:** (For boys, obviously) Dude, you're gonna start developing a mustache or a beard! Cool right? Shaving is a choice. If you choose to do it, then do it regularly and remember to clean your shaving equipment.

- **Wear Clean Clothes:** You should change your clothes, especially your underwear, daily. Your body will release fluids, and your clothes and underwear will retain those fluids causing unwanted smells. Your socks should also be changed daily to prevent smelly feet. Yuck!
- **Wash Hands Often:** Germs can quickly spread with unclean hands. Wash your hands when you get home from an outing, before/after you eat, and after using the washroom.
- **Nail Care:** Taking care of ourselves includes cleaning and regularly filing/cutting nails. You might like your nails long, though long nails are breeding grounds for germs. Grab a nail brush to scrub out the dirt regularly. Also, try to avoid bad habits like fingernail biting.

There are a TON of options in the market to help you stay clean. There are marketing ploys to buy the latest and greatest to keep your face free of zits and have a clear complexion. It might take a few purchases to find what you like. But try to get through the product's end before buying the next one. Sometimes, it takes time for our bodies to adjust and to see what we like/don't like.

General Tips

Choose a face wash that's right for your skin. You can use the tips of your fingers to create gentle, circular motions with the product around your entire face.

Your skin needs some love in the form of moisturizers. Apply moisturizer to keep your skin hydrated and prevent wrinkles. If you have oily skin, shoot for the oil-free moisturizers. If you have acne, use gel-based ones, and if you have sensitive skin, avoid moisturizers with fragrances.

Once a week, exfoliate your face and body. Using a homemade scrub is best - no need to scrub too hard. Your skin is sensitive, so go for what's gentle. A simple home scrub recipe is made up of sugar and honey. Scrub gently and rinse off with water.

It might feel nice, but avoid showering in hot water. Hot water will dry out your skin, scalp, and hair.

Trim your hair every 6 weeks, no matter what type of hair texture or length you have. This keeps your hair healthy and strong.

Use gentle products on your hair. Stay away from products with harsh chemicals like sulfates, silicones, parabens, and so on.

Keep your nails short and filed. Long nails get dirty quickly and can lead to the temptation of biting them.

Tips For Gals

Hey Ladies, I know precisely how this phase feels because I've been there. You want to look attractive, and how you care *for your body* makes a big difference in how you carry *yourself*. Here are some tips to support you.

- **Moisturize Before A Shower:** Apply coconut or olive oil to moisturize before getting into the shower. You'll create a barrier between your skin and the shower water, preventing the skin from drying out faster.
- **Avoid Heating Tools:** Styling/Heating tools can be harmful to your hair. Try not to go for styles that involve using them; if you have to, apply a protective serum.
- **Limit Hair Coloring:** Products that change your hair color can be harsh, so experimenting often with your hair color can damage your hair. If you really fancy it, then do it just twice a year.
- **Protect Your Hair:** You need protection from harsh sunlight, salt, and chlorine from swimming pools. Use a swim cap when getting in the water, and wear a hat on super sunny days.

Smokey eyes and glossy lips, please bring out the makeup! Younger gals wanna look older, while older women wanna look younger! Here are some beauty/makeup tips:

- **Moderation is Key:** Applying too much makeup can definitely be a makeup fail. It's best left for the stages and steals your natural beauty. Be moderate when trying out makeup tricks. Always remember less is more, and simplicity is perfection.
- **Watch for Sensitivity:** Some skin is susceptible and could react to various products. So be mindful and always test out samples of products before using them.
- **Remove Makeup:** Always wipe your makeup off before you go to bed. Invest in a gentle cleanser for this, or grab some coconut oil and a cotton pad. Remember to be gentle!
- **Let Skin Breathe:** Believe it or not, you really don't need foundation at this stage. Makeup in your teens should just be a bit of mascara and lip balm/gloss. Plastering on the foundation and rouge can also have the opposite effect you desire and actually GIVE you pimples by blocking your pores.

Tips For Guys

Hey, Dudes! Grooming and skincare are for more than just the ladies. You've got to get into a steady routine also. And just in case you're wondering why bother - it's because you want to preserve your handsomeness. Obviously.

- **Wear Deodorant:** Body odor kicks in as you begin to experience puberty. Thankfully, some wise person invented deodorants. Find deodorants with 100% naturally-derived ingredients. And if you want to go a step further, you can opt for ones that include scents.

- **Find Your Scent:** One scent, though, k? And not gallons of it! You can experiment with different smells and find what you like, but please stick to one scent. Don't use deodorant that smells one way and a cologne that smells different. And don't over-scent. You might *think* you need more than one spray. Trust me. You don't.
- **Grooming Facial Hair:** Facial hair grows in different lengths and speeds for guys. If yours is coming in partially, there is no point trying to 'rock it' like it's full. Just relax and give it time to grow. A clean look is not a bad look! If you have full facial hair, trim it, shave it, and keep it looking tidy. Invest in a good beard trimmer, shaving stick, or electric shaver.
- **Cleanse and Moisturize:** Look for products formulated for men and use those. No, cleansers and moisturizers are not only a girl's thing!

Kim's Corner: *Acceptance is Key!*

Everyone goes through puberty at different times, which means everyone's body changes at different paces. This also means hormones affect you and your peers in different ways. Listen, I promise you when I say that **everyone** is worried about what other people think on some level. Do your best to focus on yourself and accept where you are now. Things will change and won't stay the same for long in this short phase of life.

If you think something negative about someone else and THEIR hygiene habits, please refrain from saying anything to them.

If you come in contact with someone in class who smells funny, has bad breath, or has dirty nails, please let it be. There is absolutely NO need to make a point out of this, especially in front of anyone else. Trust me. They are going through their own process of discovering themselves. Bringing this up in an embarrassing way can have detrimental effects on that individual.

Be kind, ok? We're all human. And everyone is on a different journey, with diverse backgrounds and cultures. Just accept who they
are. You worry about yourself and let them worry about themselves.

If this is a friend and you're comfortable saying something, there's
always a way of being kind. For example, you might want to let your
friend know they have something in their teeth after lunch. But be
discreet, and tell them quietly so as not to embarrass them in a
group setting. Make sense?

FOUR

Healthy Habits

W hat's a Habit, anyways? A habit is a routine behavior that is repeated regularly and tends to occur subconsciously.

Chances are you've picked up different habits - from peers, media, parents, and so on - some good, others... not-so-good. I'll focus on the best practices for your physical health; what you consume, how you stay active, and how well you sleep.

Let's Talk Nutrition!

Proper nutrition gives your body all the right nutrients to function optimally. You eat right, your body works right, and you feel right. Simple, right?

You've probably heard this before - but I'm gonna say it. *You've only got one body, so you must look after it!*

Benefits of Proper Nutrition

Here's why it only makes sense to be mindful of what you eat.

. . .

Weight Management

You're likely to maintain a healthier weight when you make the right food choices. Your teen years are filled with physical changes, including growth spurts (which means you might be hungry more!). Making wholesome choices will actually let you eat more while keeping your weight at a healthy gauge.

Reduces Risk of Diseases

Diseases are real, y'all! And no, they don't just happen to older people. Having proper nutrition keeps your body happy and strong so you can be at your best to fight off disease.

Boosts your Immune System

I know it's fun to fake sick and stay home from school every once in a while. But when you're really ill, it's a different story. No one likes being sick and feeling weak. When you eat right, your body is strong and is able to fight off illness much more effectively.

Increased Energy

Good nutrition from healthy eating (and exercise, which we'll talk about in a bit) helps to keep your energy levels up so you can continue having fun in all your activities.

Slows Aging

Get this! Want to avoid looking like you're 38 when you're only 18? Proper nutrition is the place to start maintaining your youthful look.

Better Skin (less zits!)

I know it seems like the absolute worst thing that could happen to you - that giant zit that just showed up outta NOwhere right before the first day of class. Ugh... By eating healthy, you will have clearer and healthier skin.

Helps Focus

Sugary treats or sodas don't have any good calories or nutrients. And while calories are needed for energy, when they lack nutritional value, it's actually way worse for you. Fuel your mind and body with nutritious foods instead,

Supports Mental Health

When you eat right, you feel right. Nutritious foods support a clean body. And this helps to keep your mind clear.

As a teen, you need extra nutrients to support bone growth, hormonal changes, and other physical development, including the brain. Do your best to limit highly processed food, sugary drinks, and eating out. And remember to eat breakfast, drink water, and choose healthier food and snacks.

Tips for Daily Nutrition!

Breakfast is crucial! School may get increasingly challenging as you grow older. Not having breakfast can result in low concentration in class and cause you to be irritable. Nobody loves being around a *hangry* teenager!

Understanding calories can seem a bit complicated, but they aren't. You don't need to go all ninja on food labels, but if you consciously avoid foods high in saturated fats and refined sugars, you should be just fine.

Consuming too many calories can lead to unwanted weight gain. On the flip side, eating too little leads to fatigue, a reduced natural ability to fight illnesses, and long-term hormonal issues.

Eat most of your meals during your most active periods. Don't be tempted to eat heavy meals or processed snacks late at night. (Avoid ordering pizza late at night while you're studying.) If you have reasons to stay up late, shoot for healthy snacks like nuts and fruits or a protein smoothie.

Stay hydrated! Water is the absolute best drink of choice for you. Sometimes the body is dehydrated, but you may read it as hunger. Before you take that extra serving at dinner, consider chugging down some water and giving it 10 minutes. Likely, you'll have eaten enough!

Exercise is Wise!

You've undoubtedly heard it before - exercise is good for you! And it's true! It also helps you feel good and gives you more energy.

No matter your background or circumstance, you've got to focus on being active because it's important for your overall health.

Do I mean sweating your buns off each day?? Not necessarily. You need about 60 minutes of moderate to intense physical activity daily. Yup, you read that right - DAILY. But you can easily achieve this. Exercise has so many benefits for your health. Let's go through a few reasons to stay active.

Boosts your Mood

Hello, happiness; goodbye, sadness! Studies show a strong link between exercise and how you feel. Hormones elevate when you exercise - endorphins, oxytocin, dopamine, and serotonin. The combination of these hormones helps to promote happiness and pleasure and reduce anxiety and depression.

Good for the Brain

When you exercise, blood circulation is optimized through your brain, which means you'll think better and faster! In other words, exercising can support your ability to study well for that math test and help you smash your GED. Somebody bring out the dumbbells, please!

Weight Management

I mentioned this with nutrition, and it certainly applies to exercise. When you exercise, you burn calories, and burning *adequate* calories helps you maintain a healthy weight and improve your health conditions.

Muscle Tone

Whether you want well-toned arms, legs, and butt, or ripped arms and abs... you gotta get *working* and be active! Exercise will tone your body's muscles and support a healthy fat-to-muscle ratio that makes you fitter, stronger, and even more attractive. Wink!

Reduces Risk

Regular exercise reduces the risk for certain conditions like type II diabetes, stroke, heart disease, and cancer. It lowers your blood pressure while increasing good cholesterol in your body. This is good!

Age Gracefully

As you age, your bones shrink in density and size, get weaker, and your muscles lose their youthful strength and flexibility. OK, so you still have LOTS of time before this occurs. But regular exercise will strengthen your bones and delay bone loss. Woot!

Lifestyle Choices

Right now, you might feel the joy and excitement of an independent life beginning. You're working to gain freedoms that you've never experienced up to now. Maybe you can choose your food, decide if you'll go out or stay in, walk, bike, or grab a ride somewhere...

Life is full of lots of choices. And now is the absolute BEST time for you to make sound, long-term lifestyle choices, which will benefit you for years to come (promise!). Let's get to it...

Choose Activity

If you're close enough to school, walk or bike when you can instead of hopping in a vehicle. Walk the dog! Use the stairs instead of an elevator. While waiting for the bus, stand up instead of sitting down. (And if you're really ambitious, you could do some squats or stretches while you wait.)

Cut Screen Time

Because this usually means you're sitting down. If you can stand while using a computer, awesome! If you're watching TV, take a walk to the kitchen to get water in between commercial breaks. Bust a few dance moves between your series of binge-watching sessions. Do a few jumping jacks, push-ups, and burpees.

Join a Gym

Many gyms have start-up deals that can be pretty affordable. And then get to the gym 1-3 times a week.

Join a Sports Team

Most schools offer organized teams you can join, like football, volleyball, and track and field. Give something a try, even if you've never done it before. You can also join local teams that don't require tryouts. Many cities offer teams like soccer and softball, which you can play for fun and are less competitive.

Get Creative at Home

There are many ways to work your muscles at home; play tug of war with older siblings (or your dog?). Jump rope is tons of fun and a great form of cardio. All you need is a rope and a little outdoor space. You could follow fitness influencers on social media and do body weight, resistance bands, and dumbbell exercises virtually. Climb trees and playground equipment. Get creative about what's around you, and get active!

Help your Folks

Be helpful to mom and dad by mowing the lawn and doing house chores (more on this in the next chapter). If sweeping is gonna get your heart moving, then why not? Help wash the car in the drive-way, rake the leaves, take out the trash… get it?

Discover physical activities that you enjoy. That way, you are more likely to continue being active into adulthood. Do your best to make healthy, happy, and lasting Lifestyle choices now!

The Deal With Diets

Dieting has become popular with teens, especially girls. The truth is that social media, TV, movies, magazines, posters, and ads significantly influence what *looking good* means. These agencies also lead the conversations around how cool*ness* can be attained and what particular body type, size, or structure defines beauty/handsomeness.

Additionally, friends and even family members can reinforce these things, sometimes without meaning to. These contribute to a dissatisfied perception of one's body image, causing unhealthy relationships with food and exercise.

The strongest message conveyed is ... *you should be thin if you're female and have a lot of muscles if you're male. And by the way - you shouldn't have ANY body fat, ok? Oh ya, and if you achieve this feat, you'll be more attractive, happy, and in control too!*

Hogwash!!!

In real life, happy and successful people come in all shapes and sizes. Period.

Ironically, suppose an unhealthy attachment to changing body image is the motivation. In that case, such a teen may start exercising or eating well, but their intention is focused in the wrong place. This teenager could become overly cautious of what they eat to the point of obsession or anxiety.

They may work out intensely multiple times a day to burn extra calories. They might skip meals and restrict consuming enough good calories... all of this could develop into a full-blown eating disorder in adulthood. Eating disorders pose significant risks to your mental and physical health.

And guys, if you think you should use protein powder to add in calories to help your muscles get bigger, many of these mixtures are filled with things that really aren't healthy for your growing body.

Please talk to a professional before you buy a special powdered promise.

When diets are started due to personal insecurity, it can contribute to depression and low self-esteem. This is because dieting is mainly based on your physical body rather than how you *feel* about your body.

Dieting in itself isn't always harmful. It means being mindful of what you're eating for a period of time to get a particular result. But there are LOTS of caveats to this... And unless you've been instructed by a health professional to watch your weight, you shouldn't have to diet in your teens.

If you are overweight, speak with a licensed professional like your doctor, a personal trainer, or a dietitian so they can recommend a sustainable approach for your overall health.

Food is energy and **fuels** the body. Exercise, when done safely, **improves** your body. In plain terms... If you eat right, your body works right, and you'll feel right.

Get your ZZZZZZZ's

I can't talk about healthy habits without mentioning sleep. Proper sleep is so important! It's vital to overall health and is highly underrated.

You're in a period of increased mental, emotional, and physical growth. Getting adequate sleep is critical to this growth. When you sleep, your brain is still very much at work. It's regenerating many body parts so you can function optimally.

You need somewhere between 9 and 10 hours of sleep each night. That might seem like a lot, but it's very achievable with the following tips:

- Avoid caffeinated products after mid-afternoon (coffee, tea, energy drinks, etc.)

- Don't rely on herbal teas or sleeping meds to get you to sleep. Use natural remedies instead, like a warm bath or an aromatherapy oil diffuser with a gentle scent like lavender.
- Avoid screen time before bedtime. The blue light from your phone or laptop's screen can make it more difficult to fall asleep.
- Don't overschedule your days. School activities already take up a large part of your weekdays, and your mind needs some downtime too. Leave some space for weekend fun, which supports your overall wellness.
- Have a bedtime routine. Try a night shower, write in a journal, read a little, and try a relaxing stretch routine. Allow yourself to get sleepy before crawling into the sheets.
- Exercise is great, but avoid intense workouts in the evening. Working out at a high intensity in the evening can make it difficult for your body to settle into sleep mode at night.

It can take some consciousness to look after your health. But I promise it's worth it - your body will support you for many decades, so it's time to start taking care of it. Have a well-rounded plan to get active, eat well, stay hydrated, and sleep well.

I will always advocate for healthy habits - eat right, exercise regularly, and get good sleep. This supports a healthy state of mind.

Kim's Corner: *Truth Bomb on Drugs & Alcohol*

These years are filled with exploration - I get it! Many teens want to experiment with alcohol and drugs at some point.

The thing is, you really need to understand the risks associated with excessive drinking or drugs. It can be dangerous and have terrible lasting repercussions.

Drugs and alcohol attack every part of your body and are not good for you. You've heard that before. During your teen years, your body goes through a LOT. Too much drinking and experimenting with certain drugs can severely affect your mental, emotional and physical health.

Your brain is still developing, and experimenting can quickly graduate into dependency. Once that happens, you become susceptible to all sorts of health risks that could take a lifetime to recover.

It might seem like a good idea at the moment, but drugs and alcohol are suppressors.

Despite some uninhibited good times, when the fun is over, you're left feeling depressed and unmotivated. This can cause anxiety and depression and lead to self-harming behaviors.

There are lots of other side effects, too, like impaired judgment, dizziness, liver damage, strokes, and memory loss. Using drugs and drinking alcohol weakens your immune system. They cause various cardiovascular conditions, including abnormal heart rate, heart attacks, liver failure, ulcers, seizures, infertility, and brain damage.

Ugh, the list just goes on…

Additionally, some drugs, like meth, crack, cocaine, and heroin, are incredibly addictive. You might think once is just fun, but because your brain is still developing, the addictive impact is far, FAR greater now. Please don't touch these.

Here's the thing. You're a teen, and the odds are pretty high that you'll choose to try some things no matter what you know about them. I'm not telling you not to experiment here and there. However, I strongly suggest you wait until you're older and make safe and responsible choices.

Lastly, if you put ANY booze in your mouth, please NEVER get behind the wheel of a car. And never ride with anyone who's been drinking. Capisce??

FIVE

Tidying The Turf

I f you live with mom and dad, I imagine you've fantasized about the day you move out on your own. Ahhhhh Independence!! How lovely!

Now… how you thrive while *still living* with your parents will to a great extent, reflect how you'll succeed when you live on your own.

Keeping your space clean is essential to growing up and being an adult. So here in this chapter, we'll discuss keeping your home tidy. This refers to whatever environment you're currently in. It could be that you're already in your own rented flat, or it could also mean *your room* in your parents' home. Either way, it's time to take responsibility for your space, and this chapter is for you.

What's the point?

You may think tidying up is simply doing your parents a favor, and it's that, yes… but it's also a skill that prepares you for the real world of independence.

Here's the main gist. When you live independently, you've gotta tidy the turf!

Whether conscious of it or not, the physical space you live in, which may be your room right now, plays an important role in your behavior. This is because your mind cannot live entirely independently of your environment. If your room is untidy, it affects your state of mind, and you might feel more stressed out, anxious and struggle to sleep soundly. Simply put, a tidy room equals a tidy mind.

Keeping a tidy home comes with many health benefits! The more organized and peaceful your space is, the calmer and more together you'll feel, even if you're not fully conscious of it.

In addition, your social life can be made or marred by how tidy (or not) your home/room is. If you have a dirty, smelly room, will you invite someone in? Doubtful! On the other hand, when your space is clean, you're ready for company anytime.

Prep-Talk

For some reason, the *responsibility* of having to do the cleaning makes it harder. As if the word 'chore' makes us instantly pull back and resist. But really, cleaning doesn't have to be so bad.

Here are some ways you might consider preparing to clean.

Plan It

Block the time off so you don't make plans or forget. This also helps you mentally prepare for the task.

Cleaning Wears

Having particular clothing for cleaning prepares your brain for the work ahead. Throw on some items you don't mind getting dirty.

Get your Groove On

A fun-loving music playlist helps every single time! Dance and sing out loud, and you will literally forget that it's a chore you're carrying out.

. . .

Set Timers

Map out cleaning sections, and set a timer to encourage you toward the finish line.

Open Windows

Let fresh air in during the day (and let the bad odor escape). Fresh air cleanses the home, so create a draft if you can while you're cleaning.

Declutter

Take this opportunity to donate items you don't want or need any longer. You may realize you have too many clothes, shoes, books, or games. As you clean, put these aside to make space in your room.

Reward

When you get through the cleaning, remember to reward yourself because you deserve it!

Kitchen Cleanup

In an earlier chapter, we talked about how important the kitchen is. So much happens here… it's likely the room you're in the most, other than your bedroom. So let's go over some easy ways to straighten up here.

1. First things first … Clear the counters of anything that doesn't belong. Tidy up the clutter. You know, all the books and clothes that end up on the tables and counters.
2. Put dirty dishes in the dishwasher or a sink full of warm, soapy water.
3. Wipe off the countertops and tables to get rid of dust and stains. You can use a kitchen disinfectant that will kill bacteria.
4. Next, wash the soaked dishes in the sink, if any.
5. Clean any food scraps out of the sink and wipe down the faucets.

6. Sweep the floor and dry dust any rugs.
7. Empty the trash. Boom! All done!

Clean An Oven

Most homes will have an oven. And if you ever need to move out of a home other than your parents, you'll be required to clean this out properly. Beyond a move-out, unless you're spilling food left and right in the oven, you won't need to do this one too often. But you DO want to be sure your oven is clear of food and spills to prevent a fire.

Most oven cleaners are super caustic and corrosive. Because I like to opt for more environmentally friendly options, here's the **DIY** version.

1. Ensure your oven is off and cooled, then take everything out. Grab a dishcloth, rubber gloves, baking soda, water, and add some white vinegar to a spray bottle.
2. Prepare a paste of baking soda and water. Use half a cup of baking soda and a few tablespoons of water.
3. Put on your gloves and cover the oven in the cleaning paste. Let this sit overnight or for 12 hours minimum, and wash the racks while you wait.
4. After 12 hours (or overnight), wipe it down with a damp dishcloth. You can use a spatula to scrape if there are any rough areas.
5. Next, use the spray bottle with vinegar and spritz it all over the oven's interior to ensure a sparkling, thorough clean. The vinegar reacts with the baking soda solution for deep cleaning.
6. Finally, wipe down every nook and cranny with your damp cloth to remove any remaining residue. Then add the oven racks back in!

Done! Your oven is sparkling again.

Cleaning Floors

It seems easy enough, but there are quite a number of different kinds of floors, ranging from vinyl, terracotta, quarry tiles, real wood, and laminate. These different variants require different cleaning methods.

1. To clean a vinyl surface, sweep, then wipe with a damp mop using a mild detergent mixed in the water.
2. For laminate floors, use a diluted solution of water and vinegar. Never use soap-based detergents because they're sure to leave a film on the floor. Avoid using abrasive cleaners or scouring pads, as you'll scratch the laminate. And dodge wax polishes, as they'll make your floor super slippery!
3. To clean terracotta tiles, use warm water with mild detergent. Or there are lots of special cleaners you can purchase which are perfect for cleaning these tiles. You can use a sealant and polish also.
4. The ceramic and quarry tiles need very little maintenance. Sweep and wash with a mild detergent solution before rinsing with clean water. Avoid using wax polish, or your tiles will become slippery.

As a general rule of thumb, to prevent your floor from becoming a sticky, muddy mess, sweep or vacuum it thoroughly before you add a liquid to mop it.

Someone's Gotta Do It

So I'm guessing the bathroom isn't' your most inspiring place in the home. And you may shy away from cleaning the toilet, because, well, hmm…

But when using the proper supplies, it's not so bad. And it's pretty darn quick. Use this quick process and you're done!

1. **Grab Loose Items**: Take these out of the bathroom first; towels, clothes, and products from the shower and sink… to create an easy place to clean.
2. **Dust and Sweep**: Before liquid cleaning, do a dry clean. Otherwise, you end up with big clumps of yuck. Dust the cobwebs, and sweep or vacuum the floor to remove hair and other dry dirt from the floor.
3. **Soak Shower and Bathtub:** Next, apply an all-purpose cleaner to the surfaces and let it sit.
4. **Other Surfaces:** Use an all-purpose cleaner and wipe down any towel racks, shelves, baseboards, doors, blinds, etc.
5. **Wipe Shower and Bathtub:** Because you let these soak, the hard work has already been done. Wipe and rinse! Use a glass cleaner on the shower door.
6. **Vanity Area:** Spray the all-purpose cleaner on the sink, taps, and countertops, then wipe with a clean cloth. For a soap dish or sink with build-up, use a scrubby sponge to loosen it before wiping. Wipe your mirror with a glass cleaner.
7. **The Toilet:** If you regularly scrub your toilet, simply using some all-purpose cleaner will do a great job. Just spray a bit, scrub with a toilet brush, and flush. But if there's a build-up, use a toilet bowl cleaner. When the inside is clean, spray the outside and wipe it clean.
8. **Mop:** Fill a bucket with warm water and a small amount of all-purpose cleaner. Submerge the mop but squeeze out the excess water before mopping the floor.
9. **Replace Items:** Replace all items you initially removed, wiping them if necessary. Put the trash can back and replace the freshly laundered bathmats.

It's a wrap! Cleaning your bathroom is pretty fast and simple when **regularly** following the steps above. But cleaning will take longer if you leave your bathroom and let the mess build up. Try and get to this weekly, at minimum, and you'll be amazed at how effortless it is to clean!

Make it Routine

There are 2 ways you could go here and both work. But whichever way you decide to do the cleaning, having a routine is a very good idea. And I suggest cleaning the same way, at the same time each week or day.

Option 1

Block out 90 mins to 2 hours, one day per week, that works best for you. That could be an evening or perhaps early morning. Keep it the same each week, and you'll easily keep this up.

Option 2

Create a short daily routine that gets the home cleaned over the week, in a burst of 15 - 20 mins each day. As an example;

Monday: Dust the house and clean glass and mirrors.

Tuesday: Clean the kitchen.

Wednesday: Vacuum carpets.

Thursday: Sweep and mop the floors.

Friday: Straighten up bedrooms and declutter.

Saturday: Clean the living room, playroom, or den (the main entertainment space in the home).

Sunday: Clean the bathrooms.

Kim's Corner: *Behold the Cleaning Hacks*

Let's face it, when it comes to cleaning, it just has to get done. As you take on independence, it's just part of the deal.

Because this is mandatory, I recommend you *choose* to enjoy the process and take pride in keeping a clean and organized home. I promise it will pay off in many ways over the years.

These cleaning hacks should be helpful at some point in your journey of independence.

- **Olive Oil Hack:** It's no secret that Olive oil has many nutritional benefits, but it's also a fantastic buffer for stainless steel items, like pots, pans, and alliances! Pour a tiny bit on a soft cloth and rub in a circular motion to buff out any dirty spots.
- **Lemon Hack:** You can detox the garbage disposal with lemons or limes. Cut the citrus into quarters, and while the water is running, put the lemon pieces into the disposal.
- **Alcohol Hack:** Remove carpet stains with clear alcohol (rubbing alcohol, vodka, or white wine). First, blot the stain, then pour the alcohol onto the stain. This trumps any over-the-counter product!
- **Water Spot Hack:** Depending on the number of chemicals and minerals within the water in your home taps, you may end up with water spots in your shower glass doors. Spread on some old-fashioned shaving cream and let it sit for 15 mins. Wipe off and see the new sparkle!
- **Baking Soda Hack:** Baking soda is a super way to scour the scungiest crud off practically anything in the house. Remember the oven? Mix baking soda and water together and use on the stovetop, sticky pans, ultra-dirty floors, and even the toilet bowl!
- **Nuked Sponge Hack:** Microwaves can be full of bacteria due to boiling over spills and sprays. Place a clean, reasonably damp sponge or cloth in the microwave and put it on high for 3 mins to kill the bacteria. Then wipe out the inside.
- **Glass Cleaner Hack:** Mix white vinegar, distilled water, and some drops of essential oil and shake. This is an easy and affordable way to clean your windows and mirrors.

- **Pet Hair Hack:** If your vacuum isn't quite cutting it and removing all the pet hair off your furniture etc., throw on some rubber gloves and wipe your hand over the fabric. This generates static and collects the hair. Then rinse the gloves to wash the hair away and use a drain catcher, so the hair doesn't go down the drain.

- **Dishwasher Hack:** You can use your dishwasher for lots of items other than your dishes. Try placing some of these in your machine, and get great results; rubber flip-flops, canvas sneakers, makeup brushes, plastic and rubber kids' toys, contacts lens case, mouth guards, hair brushes and combs, and refrigerator shelves…) Then sterilize your dishwasher using a cycle of straight hot water and vinegar where the solution or tablet would go.

SIX

Clothing Care & Wear

Isn't it grand when your laundry gets magically laundered, folded, and put away? (Thank you, Mom and Dad.) It's time to take this on, being more independent.

Caring for your clothes means enjoying them for longer, which has important Earth-friendly effects.

Here, we'll chat about how to care for your clothes, from laundry to simple stitching.

And long, long ago, the purpose of clothing was to stay warm and dry. But it's a different story today!

How you dress speaks volumes about you. We'll go on a wardrobe journey so you can represent yourself accurately.

Laundry 101: Understanding Labels

To care for your valued clothing, follow their labels on how to properly care for the fabric.

HOW TO WASH

MACHINE   HAND   DO NOT
WASH   WASH   WASH

1. Washing: Look for the picture of a wash bucket.

WATER TEMPERATURE

COLD   WARM   HOT
WATER   WATER   WATER

2. Wash Temperature: Look for the wash bucket with waves and dots to indicate the temperature.

CYCLE OR WASH SETTING

NORMAL   PERMANENT   DELICATE
CYCLE   PRESS CYCLE OR GENTLE
                        CYCLE

3. Washing Cycle: Notice the lines underneath the wash basket

BLEACH

BLEACHING   DO NOT   USE
ALOWED   BLEACH   NON-CHLORINE
                        BLEACH

4. Bleach: Check if your garment can handle bleach, or you may get discolored clothes.

TUMBLE DRY BASIC SYMBOL

TUMBLE   DO NOT   HANG TO
DRY   DRY   DRY

DRY   DO NOT
LAY FLAT   WIRING

5. Tumble Dry: I have shrunken too many sweaters by putting them into the dryer. Now you'll have better luck.

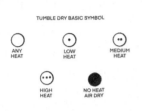

6. Tumble Temperature: Follow the little dots to indicate the ideal tumble temperature.

7. Iron: Some clothing can be damaged by heat. Check your labels before you iron.

8. Dry Clean: You only need to notice the 2 symbols here.

These symbols are fairly straightforward, just remember to check them!

Laundry 201: Sort

To get the best results, wash different colors and fabrics separately to avoid stains. You can sort clothes by color shades, fabric type or weight, and how dirty they are. Here are some sorting ideas.

a) Dark clothes bleed mostly red dye. So washing these with lighter colors can cause damage.

b) The wash cycle needed for heavy fabrics like towels differs from the cycles needed for lighter materials like silk.

c) Let's not talk about what happens if you wash items with zippers and knitted materials together! Ack!

d) If you mix extra soiled laundry with not-so-dirty laundry, one will come out improperly cleaned.

The next time you're tempted to put all your clothing into the washing machine because you have a series to return to, don't give in!

Laundry 301: Stains

Let's talk stains. It happens to the best of us. But no need to panic, you CAN get the stain out of your new shirt. But you've got to PRE-treat the stain. And if you can do this immediately, it'll be much more likely to come clean. The longer you let stains sit on your clothing, the more difficult it becomes to remove them and the more complicated the process gets. Try these methods out:

- **Coffee, Tea, Berry, Butter, Margarine, Grease, or Sweat Stains:** Pour a mild detergent directly on the stain. Then gently rub the fabric together and leave it on for a few minutes. You can also use a cleaning toothbrush to help the detergent get into the stain.
- **Blood, Dirt, or Motor Oil Stains:** Mix a small amount of water and detergent. Let your stained clothes soak for about 30 minutes before washing them.
- **Chewing Gum Stains:** Test a discreet area of your clothes to ensure the vinegar won't ruin any color. Pour a little on and after a few mins, soak it up with a paper towel. If no color bleeds out, you're good! Then soak the affected area in hot vinegar for 1-3 minutes.

Laundry 401: Detergent

Most people waste a lot of detergent by free-pouring it into the machine. Don't do that! All laundry packaging will include instructions for the appropriate dosing, so follow the guidelines, and you can't go wrong.

Hand Wash your Fave Pieces

So based on the care label, you're meant to hand-wash your item. Here's how:

1. Fill your sink or bucket with water, and check for the appropriate water temperature based on the label.
2. Add your detergent to the water and swish. If you're unsure what detergent to use, go for mild detergents.
3. Soak your clothing in this mixture and leave it there for a few minutes.
4. Rinse and repeat. Keep changing the water as you rinse until the water is clear or the clothing is no longer slippery from the detergent. Easy Peasy!

Fix A Shrunken Sweater

At some point, you've likely experienced the deep despair of accidentally shrinking a favorite sweater item to the washer or dryer. Here are three simple steps to remedy this error. First, grab a bucket (or use a clean sink), baby shampoo, and 2 large, clean towels.

Step 1: Soak the shrunken sweater in a solution of lukewarm water and about two tablespoons of baby shampoo for 20 minutes to 1 hour.

Step 2: Don't wring! Instead, absorb water from the sweater with a towel. Lay it flat on the towel and roll it IN the towel while pressing gently. Then unroll.

Step 3: Lay the sweater on the second clean towel and stretch it to its original size by pulling gently on all sides. Then leave it there to air dry on a flat surface.

Whiten Your White Shirt

Over time, your whites might become dull or discolored. There are various ways to whiten your whites, including bleach, but I'll introduce you to three methods.

1. Distilled White Vinegar: Add one cup of distilled white vinegar to one gallon of hot water. Submerge the white clothing and let it soak overnight, then launder as usual. Add another cup of white vinegar to the rinse cycle. This will help cut through any detergent residue that leaves your clothing dull.

2. Baking Soda: Baking soda helps to deodorize and whiten your clothing. Stir half a cup of baking soda into your liquid laundry detergent. If you're using a powder detergent, add it during the rinse cycle.

3. Lemon Juice: The citric acid in lemons can bleach white clothing effectively and works well to whiten cotton, linen, and polyester fibers. Pour a cup of lemon juice into the water of your washing cycle. *Voila!*

Ironing Hacks

If you're like me, you'll do *anything* not to iron! Here are a few of my favorite ways to avoid it.

1. Avoid Ironing: When you go shopping, opt for wrinkle-resistant clothing or styles. That way, you never have to iron your clothes! Yay!

2. Use Your Dryer: I love this one! Spray your wrinkled shirt with a bit of water, and toss it in the dryer for a few minutes. The heat will smooth out the wrinkles.

3. Shower 'em Out: Place your wrinkled pants on a hanger and place them in the bathroom. Close the door and have a nice, warm shower. The steam from the bathroom will help flatten out wrinkles.

Sew it up

Sewing can be as simple as fixing a hole or putting a button back on. But it can also be complex, like sewing a gown or suit together. There's much more complexity if you want to learn to sew clothes from scratch. But to fix a seam, patch a hole or replace a button, it's pretty straightforward.

And you can start with just a needle and thread! Many different stitches exist, and I won't attempt to instruct all of these. But I'll say this.

If you can sew up and mend minor imperfections in your clothing, you'll save yourself cash, and you may just love it! It's a wonderful craft!

1. Pick a thread similar in color to the item you're mending. Unravel from the spool and snip it off.
2. Thread the needle. This takes practice, but you can wet the end of the thread to make it easier to go through the tiny hole of the needle. Pull the thread through the needle until the needle is about halfway. Next, put the two ends together (so your thread is doubled now). Tie a little knot at the end with both pieces.
3. Push the needle through the back of the garment toward the front and pull until you hit the knot. Then weave back and forth through the item until you're done!
4. Leave enough thread so you can tie off the end. Once you're done, tie a knot to wrap it up.
5. Lastly, cut any remaining thread.

What your Wardrobe Says About You

Now that we've covered clothing CARE let's turn our attention to the clothes you WEAR!

No doubt there's a lot of discovery happening for you right now. One of which may be your fashion style. Your personality is revealed to a great extent by the clothes you choose to wear.

Are you sporty? Are you a trendsetter? Do you prefer comfy, baggy clothes? The colors you wear say a lot about who you are and how you feel. Everything you wear sends a message to others.

In addition to how others see us, our clothing choices influence how we act. Consider how you feel when you get dressed up and look extra beautiful or sharp. You would carry yourself entirely differently than in sweats. Right?

Much of our drive and ambition are masked within our outfits and can give us great confidence or make us shy.

Here are some basic color representations of clothing:

RED: powerful, in control, sensual

ORANGE: energetic, vitality, happy

YELLOW: positive, lively, hopeful

GREEN: comforting, reliable, natural

BLUE: calm, successful, confidant

PURPLE: creative, royal, wealthy

BLACK: elegant, mysterious, mischievous

BROWN: dependable, wholesome, conservative

WHITE: simple, virtuous, pure

IVORY: calm, elegant, simple

Your fashion sense speaks a lot about your personality. It's an opportunity to express who you are on the inside. Be true to yourself and wear what feels good.

This may take some time to sort out. But now is a great time to develop your identity, choose your style, and rock it!

And if you need help *choosing* your style, I've got you covered!

Discover Your Style

Try these 5 steps to identify your current style.

Step 1: Audit Your Wardrobe

Categorize your clothing items and reflect on the patterns. Look for consistency! Which do you frequently wear vs. haven't worn for years? What makes you feel happy and confident? Do you wear lots of stripes or dots, abstract patterns, or is plain more your feel? Does your current wardrobe reflect your true personality? Get truthful with these questions.

Step 2: Find a Pattern

When you're done auditing your wardrobe, you'll discover your style is leaning towards a particular direction (or not). If you can find an obvious pattern, begin with what you have. What combinations can you put together? Can you add different accessories or shoes to slightly alter an outfit and keep it fresh? Cool! However, if you realize the clothing in your closet doesn't represent you accurately and needs a complete overhaul, don't fret. Just move on to the next step.

Step 3: Research Styles

The discovery that your clothes don't do you justice might cause you to *panic shop*. But wait! Instead, slow down and grab your phone or flip through magazines. Check out different fashion styles and find your preferences through *them*. You could create a Fashion Board and cut out images you fancy. You can also do this virtually or create a physical folder dedicated to your clippings. After you've spent a bit of time on this, a pattern will likely emerge, and you'll notice a preference for certain styles.

Step 4: Go Thrift

As you discover your style, you may want to try on some items that you like but might be different from what you're used to wearing. It's good to experiment, and you don't need to spend a fortune giving this a try. By shopping in your local thrift store, you'll have a chance to try different, often unique, articles.

Step 5: Three-Word Marker

This will support you when choosing new clothing for yourself. Grab a pen and paper. And write down one word for each of the following 3 questions:

- *How do you describe your style?*
- *How do you want others to describe your style?*
- *How do you want your style to make you feel?*

These three words should remain in your mind when you shop. The items you buy will be true to who you are and who you want to be seen as.

Fashion Tips

When we talk about developing a personal fashion style, it's easy to get caught up in the idea that more clothing equals more possibilities. But that's not true. Check out these ideas.

- **Get Creative:** Minimal clothing in your closet shouldn't ever be a limitation. Create combinations with what you have. Value what's in your wardrobe now and take care of each item, so it lasts.
- **Wear Clothes That Fit:** Choose clothes that fit you properly and aren't too small or large.
- **Identify Your Body Type**: You might be tall, lean, rounded with lots of muscle, average, or stockier. Identify your body type and wear clothes that sit right on your body.

- **Highlight Your Best Features:** Use clothing to show off your great features!
- **Simplicity is Key:** No need to overcomplicate your look. Pick simple, classy combinations that go well together. Remove any unnecessary or overexaggerated items.
- **Establish Your Style:** If you already have a preferred style, stick with it. But there's nothing wrong with going out of your comfort zone to spice it up. Try to be open to new things here and there.

Tie a Tie

Gents! You may need to suit up and wear a tie!

1. Drape the tie around your neck.

2. Cross the wide end over the narrow end.

3. Loop the wide end under the narrow end.

4. Loop the wide end back over again.

5. Pull the wide end up through the neck loop.

6. Insert the wide end down through the front knot.

7. Tighten the knot.

8. Tuck the narrow end of the tie into the loop on the back side of the wide end.

9. Fold your collar down, and make sure that the tie is covered by the collar around your neck. And we're done!

Tie a Tie

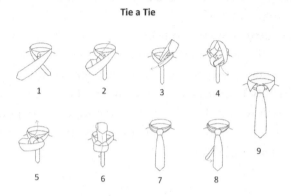

Pack a Suitcase

My grandma once gave me excellent advice. She said, "Any time you're going on a trip, lay out all the clothes you want to take with you on your bed. Then, remove half of it before packing!"

Whether it's just an overnight or a complete vacation, here are some tips to help you pack.

1. Don't Rush: If you start thinking about what you need the night before you leave, you might miss essential items. Get started early.

2. Have a List: Write out everything you think you'll need, then walk away. Then come back with a fresh mind for a review! Then tick each item off your list as they go into your suitcase.

3. Be Deliberate: Plan out each of your outfits instead of packing random *'I might need it'* pieces. Remember to check the weather where you're headed so you can pack appropriate clothes. Include articles that are versatile too, and can be worn with multiple outfits.

4. Roll your clothes: Optimize your suitcase by rolling your clothes rather than folding them.

Kim's Corner: *Say it Ain't' So!*

We live in a ThrowAway society. Often, if clothing gets ripped, it's no longer of value. Or a fashion becomes out of style, and the following new fad is in. But the truth is, discarded clothing is one of the biggest and fastest-growing environmental disasters in the World.

I will never understand why people throw clothing away, but apparently, it's prevalent. There are literally PILES of thrown-away clothing in third-world countries. The majority of fashion waste ends up in landfills.

People may think clothing will biodegrade, but it takes *decades* for most fabrics to break down. Try getting rid of your unwanted clothes in more sustainable ways. Here are some ideas.

- Mend your clothes
- Repurpose old clothes (socks into cleaning rags, pants into bags, cut an item into strips, and stuff a sagging pillow)
- Give select items to friends
- Leave some clothes outside in a bag, and label them FREE (if you live in an area where they will get taken)
- Give them away over local Freebie Facebook groups
- Bring items in good condition to consignment shops
- Donate them to charity or thrift stores

SEVEN

Handy In The Home

W hether you're already living away from your parents or not - having access to these handy home skills will support you to be independent. It's also such a great help to mom and dad. If you can help them around the house with a few of these, you'll be appreciated on a whole new level!

Change a Light Bulb

In most homes, the standard is a 60 or 120-watt bulb. But there are many different wattages for varying lights, so check the watts before changing the burnt-out or damaged bulb.

Power Off: Never attempt to change a light bulb with the power still connected.

Let The Bulb Cool: Some bulbs run hot! Please wait for it to cool down so you don't get burnt! If it's an LED light bulb, you won't have this problem since it produces little to no heat.

Grab A Ladder: Light bulbs are usually placed in hard-to-reach spots. Grab a ladder when trying to replace them.

Removing Bulb

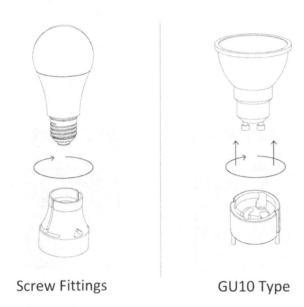

Screw Fittings   GU10 Type

Remove the Old Bulb: For screw fittings, gently twist anticlock-wise. For GU10-type fittings gently push up while turning.

Insert the Replacement: Gently push the bulb into the socket and turn clockwise until you feel it lock into place.

Power On: Switch on the power.

Dispose of old Bulb: Dispose of old light bulbs responsibly

Breakers & Fuses

Fuse Boxes and Circuit Breakers are similar. They send electricity to all areas of the home and are usually labeled as: oven, bathroom, foyer, etc. Both prevent your home and devices from overloading. The main difference between them is that fuses can't be reused, while circuit breakers can be reused over and over again. So when the fuse blows, you need to change the fuse. And if the breaker blows, you only need to switch it back on.

Breaker vs Fuse

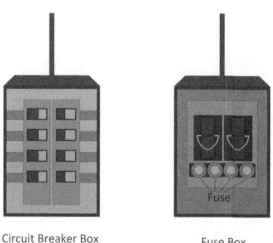

Circuit Breaker Box

Fuse Box

I recommend locating your fuse or circuit breaker box. Even if you live in your parent's home, it's just good to know. Some common areas it could be located in are the garage, attic, basement, storage, laundry, or utility room.

This may seem obvious, but please ensure your hands are dry before touching the fuse or breaker. The goal is to get you experienced, not electrocuted. If you're concerned about your safety working with a broken fuse, then don't! Contact a trained pro. It's not worth compromising yourself.

Fusebox:

1. Turn off the main power to stop the electrical flow to the fuse box.

2. Hopefully, the fuses are labeled. If not, look for the blown one. Locate the room where the outage occurred.

3. Carefully unscrew the blown fuse and replace the fuse with a new one.

Circuit Breaker:

1. Look for the tab that seems like it's in the center of the switch. Flip it to the off position.

2. Flip it back to the on position to reset the fuse.

3. Test the lights in the room that initially lost power but don't overload the circuit, or you'll end up with another blown fuse.

Clogged Sink

Have you ever had a clogged sink? Yuck! But it happens! It might be wiser to call in a plumber, depending on how severe the clog is. But on most occasions, you don't need to. Here are some DIY solutions that will help.

Method 1: Boiling Water

This method works great if you have a grease buildup. Boil a pot of water. Then slowly pour the water down the drain. Wait a few seconds between the pouring to allow the boiling water to melt the blockage. Repeat as necessary.

Method 2: Baking Soda and Vinegar

For this to work, be sure there's no standing water in the sink. Boil water and pour it down the drain. Then pour a cup of baking soda down the drain, followed by a cup of white vinegar. Plug the drain and wait about 5 to 10 minutes. Pour boiling water again. Repeat as necessary.

Method 3: Plunger

First things first... please don't use the same plunger for your toilet on your sink! It's handy to keep a smaller one around just for your sink. If you don't have a separate one, skip this method. If your dishwasher is installed and connected directly to your kitchen sink, I also wouldn't recommend this method because yucky water can get pushed into your dishwasher.

Begin by filling the sink with a few inches of water to create suction and allow the plunger to force water against the clog. Steadily plunge up and down. After several plunges, the clog should start to dissolve, and the water should begin draining. Then run the water for a few minutes to see if it flows freely.

Method 4: Drain Snake

You can use a drain snake if none of the above methods work. This is a flexible tool that bends through pipes. Begin by pushing the end into the drain and turning gently to send the snake further into the pipe. When you feel resistance, you've hit the clog. Twist and rotate the drain snake slightly to try and break it up.

Clogged Toilet

If you thought a clogged *sink* was yucky, what do you think about a clogged toilet?! Again - this happens, and probably more often than a clog in your sink. Let's talk about what you can do.

Method 1: Plunger

This method works exactly like the sink. Insert the plunger into the toilet bowl, and pump the plunger over the hole. To check the drainage, flush the toilet.

Method 2: Drain Cleaner

Heat up half a gallon of water. Pour 1 cup of baking soda and 2 cups of vinegar into the toilet. Then pour the hot water into the toilet bowl. Let the mixture stand overnight, and the clog should be dissolved by morning. If this doesn't work, then the clog is definitely not caused by an organic substance.

. . .

Method 3: Chemical Drain Cleaner

Purchase a chemical drain cleaner, available at most grocery stores, and follow the instructions. You'll need to be careful because they can have toxic fumes. Open a window if you can.

Method 4: Drain Snake

Push one end of the snake into the drain until you feel the block. Gently twist and push the snake to free up the obstruction and break it into smaller pieces that can flow through the pipes. Flush when you're confident that the block has been taken care of.

Phew! Let's move on from plungers to punctures…

Patch a Hole

It's common to find holes in the walls where you live. Nails from pictures or mirrors, as well as furniture, can cause damage to the walls. Door handles can easily create holes in the walls if the door is slammed open and there's no door stopper.

Fixing a hole in drywall takes little time or experience. If the hole is pretty small, all you'd need is a drywall compound and a putty knife. Some compounds will be pink in the package, then dry white. So you'll always know when it's dry.

Spread the putty thinly over the hole using the special flat putty knife. Once it's dry, you can use a small piece of sandpaper to smooth it out. If the hole is large, like a door handle size, fill the gap with something to insulate, like a paper bag. Push the bag into the hole, so it doesn't stick out. Then cover the hole with drywall compound. Once it's completely dry, sand it smooth, then paint over the patch. Boom! You're done!

Painting Basics

Painting can be super fun! A painting challenge can be a great way to bond with friends or siblings. But remember to give yourself enough time for the entire project. The amount of time required will vary based on the size of your room, the type of paint, how you're painting, and your skill level. Some spaces can take just a few hours, while others can take several days. Take your time, and enjoy the process!

Before you pick up that paintbrush, you want to think some aspects through *first*. It's best to have a plan and enroll everyone involved.

The Look

Start with how you want the finished room to look. What color will it be? Will it be more than one color? Pick up a few paint swatches from the paint store, where you can bring them home and compare the colors.

Attire

Be sure you have comfortable clothing (and shoes) you are okay getting paint on. If you don't have anything, pop into a local thrift shop and grab something.

Gear Up

The tools vary depending on *where* you're painting and what kind of paint you use. However, some essentials are handy no matter what type of walls are being painted!

- Paint
- Paint roller
- Paint roller extension pole
- Drop cloths
- Paint brushes
- Paint tray
- Sandpaper
- Painter's tape
- Rags
- Putty knife

Purchase Paint

Calculate how much paint you'll need. If you're painting a small room, you only need a small can. Try and determine your square footage and ask the retailer.

Prep the Room

Remove items from the room that could get paint on them. If you can't move large pieces of furniture, ensure they're covered using drop sheets. If you don't have enough space to empty the room, push things to the center and protect them.

Tape

Ensure there's no dust on your walls, then apply painting tape to create straight edges and prevent overspill.

Mix your Paint

Paint separates, so use a wooden paint stick to stir the paint. And stir periodically throughout the painting project.

Technique

Once your paint is mixed and your roller is ready, start from the ceiling down. I like to get the corners of the walls first with a brush, then go crazy with a roller on the larger surfaces.

Ventilate

Having proper airflow in the painted area will speed up the drying process, and it's vital for safety as paint fumes are strong and can be toxic. Open windows and use fans.

Clean

Clean up while the paint is still wet. Otherwise, your paint brushes, tray, and anything else paint is smeared on will be much harder to clean. For latex and water-based paints, wash the brushes with soapy water. For oil-based paints, use paint thinner. And... you're a painter, Woot!

Lawn Care

Looking after the lawn is a great way to get involved around the home. This could be moving the yard, raking the leaves, or pruning trees or bushes.

It's physical work, brings you outside, and is a typical first job for many teens. But take proper safety measures before you operate these machines and consult an adult.

Know your Machine

Read the manual if you can! Yep, it's not the most exciting read. This will help you understand the safest way to use your machine. Many models will operate differently, some on gas, some on electricity.

Prep the Space

Walk the area you're about to mow. Remove sticks, rocks, and other debris from the lawn that may be struck by the machine. If these get thrown out by the mower, someone could get injured.

Dress the Part

Wear proper boots that cover your toes and ankles and durable pants (yes, even in the summer) to protect your legs. Grab safety glasses to shield your eyes and use earplugs to safeguard against prolonged exposure to loud engine noises. And always wear gloves.

Know the Risk

Lawnmowers and weed trimmers can get extremely hot. The engine is out in the open, so be mindful not to touch it. And keep your gloves on, even when you stop moving, as the machine could still be very hot for a while. When adding fuel, triple-check that there are no ignition sources such as cigarettes. Maintain a safe distance from running mowers, especially if you're a passerby. Flying debris can be ejected and cause significant damage. And if the mower stops working because it hit a stick or got stuck on something, NEVER reach in with your fingers to dislodge it. The blades may suddenly spin again if there is any stored energy. Just don't ever reach in for any reason, ok? It's not worth the risk of injury.

If you're between 13 and 16, please only operate a riding lawn mower with proper instruction and supervision. And never carry any passenger on a riding mower. Accidents can happen suddenly. Stay safe by following these tips, and you'll surely have a beautiful lawn!

Home Safety

Being security conscious is one of the hallmarks of adulthood. Whether living with your folks or renting your own place, secure your home and keep your belongings safe.

Create a security routine that you do regularly before leaving home.

1. Ensure the stove burners are off and unplug appliances which could overheat.
2. Close and lock your windows.
3. Keep valuables out of sight and hide keys, including car keys. (A trained thief could hook keys or valuables through even a tiny opening.)
4. Don't leave ID in obvious places like the entrance shelf.
5. Shut the curtains and leave some lights on if you return after dark.
6. Set your alarm if you have one.
7. Lock the side gate, shed, and garage.

If you're going away for a while, it's always better to leave the impression you're still home.

Try these to protect your home.

1. Don't post anything on social media about leaving. If you do, ensure your posts aren't public and are viewed only by friends.

2. Leave lights and a TV on a timer to make your home seem lived in.
3. Invite a trusted neighbor to keep an eye on your place and pick up the mail.
4. You could even ask your neighbor to periodically park in your driveway.
5. Cancel regular deliveries like newspapers or food bins, so your entrance doesn't give you away.

Kim's Corner: *When to call it in...*

I spent some time explaining many 'do-it-yourself' maintenance ideas in this chapter. That's great for the most part; you can often save some big bucks. But it's also good to understand *when* to call in the pros.

If you're dealing with anything gas related, for example. Don't attempt to go to the furnace room and mess with things. Call your natural gas company. If you smell a rotten egg scent, please go out of the house and call emergency services, as this could be a gas leak.

If you need electrical work, it's super easy to get hurt if you're unsure precisely what to do. Please call an electrician. And if you end up with a clog in your pipes and you're not comfortable trying some of the above methods, it's perfectly ok to call in a plumber.

Sometimes, more damage can be caused by trying to fix something on our own when it should be left to an expert. If something happens in your home, call your folks, if possible. They will likely be able to guide you to the safest way of handling a situation.

EIGHT

Getting Around with Transit Town

A necessary part of becoming independent is your ability to get around on your own. Likely, you'll use transit before you consider your own vehicle. And there are lots of benefits to using public transit.

You get to chill, listen to music, read a book and let someone else take you where you need to go for a small fee.

It's an efficient and conscientious method of transportation. Consider the greenhouse gas emissions and air pollution if everyone who uses transit were to drive instead. It's also more affordable than using and maintaining a vehicle. Plus, you can even get some work or studying done while traveling. And if you're into it, it's a neat opportunity to meet new people.

Depending on your country, you'll encounter various kinds of transit. You'll have to check your city's website to see what's available. City buses and taxis are the most common types in most countries. But many others exist (and are fun to use). There are trolley buses, trams, rapid transit (which includes metro and subway lines), ferries, bicycles, tricycles, scooters, and even motorcycles!

How It Works

Let's go through some key aspects to consider when you take public transit.

1) Find Your Route

Public transportation vehicles have set routes that they travel on. And they repeat the pattern all day long. Grab yourself a map, look online, or call the transit service to figure out where to get on and off so you get where you need to go. If you have the map or look online, you can view the timetables there. Look for the route closest to where you need to be.

2) Fares

Each city and region has its own fare system. Often one base fare can include your entire trip, but not always. If you need to ride on a bus then a ferry, for example, it's possible you need to pay one fare for the bus and then an additional fare for the ferry. Check this out before heading on your journey.

Other than the city bus, where you can pay ON the bus, for the most part, you would buy your fare card from a machine outside of the transit station. Once you've paid your fare, you enter the paid area to catch your ride. You should be able to use cash, debit, or credit to buy the initial card.

For buses, you may be able to use change to pay your fare. But many transit systems are equipped to accept prepaid cards only. Be sure where you're going so you purchase the correct fare before you enter the paid area.

Some transit systems, like buses, won't necessarily spit out a new card if you pay your fare on board with cash. And if your journey includes another bus, you will need a 'transfer slip.' Remember to ask for one when you get in, or you could be asked for a new fare when you get on the next bus.

In addition to paying each time you ride, there are other ways to pay your fare. You can invest in a monthly or daily pass, so you don't need to calculate the exact fare required for each trip. You just hop on!

3) Ride

When boarded, look for an open seat and get comfortable. Sometimes, you may not find a seat if it's busy. If this happens, stand someplace as out of the way as possible. You don't want to get pushed or shoved over by accident.

Public transit can get crowded, especially at peak times. Try to be considerate and accommodating. If you're standing, keep your backpack close to free up room for others. If you're sitting, hold your bag rather than let it take up a seat next to you. If someone boards who needs a seat, like a person who has low vision, is in a wheelchair, or is elderly, it's kind to stand and give them your seat. Please be courteous.

Once you approach your stop, press the button or pull a rope to signal the driver for an intended stop. The exit is usually through the back door. If you need to cross the road right away, give the bus a moment to drive off before heading out on the street so you can view the entire road.

Public Transportation Safety

- **Stay Connected:** Let a parent know when you're taking transit and your intended route. Tell them when you leave and let them know when you arrive at your destination.
- **Plan your Route:** There are lots of apps to help with this that will show you, in real time, where you are in relation to where you're going. It's tough to get lost using one of these apps, and I recommend downloading one on your phone for your city.

- **Know your Exits:** Always scan for possible exits. Check where the nearest exits, fire exists, and alarms are in case you need to get off quickly.
- **Stay Visible:** I'm not saying public transportation is full of crazy people. However, there are people in transit who you probably want to avoid. So, as a rule, avoid sitting in an empty carriage. If you are traveling by bus after dark, sit near the driver.
- **Stay Alert:** Don't let yourself get too distracted by other things. Lack of attention can make you an easy target.
- **Use a Licensed Cab:** This is safer than ride-hailing services like Uber or Lyft. Taxi drivers have stricter employment standards and comprehensive background checks. If you take a non-conventional ride, please ensure the details on your app match the details of the car (and driver!).
- **Secure Valuables:** Keep your bag right under your armpits. It can get crowded on public transit, something thieves wield to their advantage. The busier the place, the more conscious of your environment you should be.
- **Trust your Instincts:** If you're sitting somewhere and feel uneasy or uncomfortable, change your location or alert the driver. Your gut might pick up on something you can't even see.
- **Report It:** If you see something suspicious, don't hesitate to alert a member of the station's staff or call the police. It could be nothing, but it never hurts to be cautious.

Carry Cash

This little tip could save you in a bind. I believe in carrying a little cash all the time in case of unexpected situations. In a World where we mostly use plastic cards, it's still possible that you'll need to use cash, especially if there's no access to a bank (or your parents) or if internet systems go down.

I don't mean carrying a lot of cash. You wouldn't want to lose it. But even a $20 bill is a good safety precaution. And like the Scouts say, "Be prepared!" Here are a few reasons you want to keep a bit of cash money around:

1. **Emergency:** Never say never! You never know what can happen. Whether you're heading on a trip, meeting with friends, or just taking a walk, having cash at hand is an important safety tip.
2. **Split Bills:** Eating out with friends? Instead of having the restaurant print separate bills, throw some cash to your buddy who paid the bill.
3. **Envelope System:** This one is great for saving. If you place a bit of cash in an envelope each week, it will add up quickly, and you'll have a bunch of cash for a rainy day at some point. Or, if you need to leave the house quickly, you can grab a quick bill from here instead of having to stop by the bank.

Kim's Corner: *So what do you DO on transit?*

Depending on how long you need to be traveling, you may need to avoid boredom. Here are some ideas:

- **Read:** Many stations have free newspapers or magazines. You can learn a lot from browsing the many publications out there. You can also read your fav book for the ride!
- **Listen to an Audiobook:** Try listening instead to a good book or a subject you're interested in.
- **Learn a Language:** Spend your time learning a language.
- **Study:** Use the time to study for class or memorize something you need to know in an area you're interested in.
- **Journal:** Jot down goals and how you can achieve them. I enjoy writing down my thoughts and feelings. Just get introspective and write!

- **Plan:** Make a to-do list!
- **Think:** There are many things to contemplate in life. Use the time to consider and think critically about something you find fascinating.
- **Meditate:** A great time to concentrate on your breathing and focus inward.
- **Puzzles:** You can get puzzle books, an excellent way to pass the time and a great way to exercise your brain.
- **Chill:** Simply enjoy looking out the window at the changing scenery, or people watching.
- **Chat:** If you like, you can talk to people around you. Most often, people are quiet in transit and keep to themselves. But occasionally, if you're feeling it and it's appropriate, you could start a conversation with someone. There's nothing wrong with a little friendly, harmless conversation, especially with an elderly rider. It's so lovely for them.

NINE

Your Own Wheels

I think it's pretty safe to say owning a car is many a teen's dream! If you are fortunate enough to buy one, you'll also need to be ready for the responsibilities. Let's get into it!

Choose a budget

The first step to buying a car is figuring out how much you can afford. Unfortunately, there's no secret formula because only you can determine what makes the most sense for your financial situation.

Consider the following as a guide to help you make the right choice.

- **Total Price:** The 'sale price' you see for the vehicle will differ from the actual price you'll pay. Additional expenses could include sales taxes, registration fees, and documentation fees. You may also consider an extended warranty, especially for a used car. Talk to the dealership about the *total* cost rather than just the vehicle cost.
- **Maintenance:** The vehicle itself can sometimes be the most affordable part of car ownership! We'll discuss this in

more detail later, but when you consider a vehicle purchase, understand the upkeep costs to have one.

- **Insurance:** There's no way around this. There are insurance fees if you want to be on the road.
- **Down Payment:** A larger payment upfront minimizes borrowing. This also means you pay less interest over the life of the loan, and you benefit from lower monthly payments.
- **Monthly Payment:** Determine what you can afford each month and how long. Consider the length of the loan term and interest rate, which adds to the principal balance. Be sure you can comfortably take this on and complete the agreement.
- **Trade-In:** If this isn't your first vehicle, you could trade in your old ride at the dealership. The vendor will assess your car and give you an amount of money you can put toward a different vehicle.

Choose The Right Car

You and your car will be friends for a while! You want to choose one that suits your needs all year round and for years to come. Once you determine a budget, you can start looking for vehicles within that budget. But the market is filled with opportunities, so where do you start?

1. Assess your Needs: Determine what you'll primarily use the car for. For many teens, a hatchback or small 4-door sedan works great.

2. Lease or Buy: There are a few ways to drive a car off the lot. You can buy the vehicle by paying the total outright or finance the total cost with monthly payments. A vehicle can also be leased, which is like borrowing a car from a dealership. You must have good credit to qualify for a lease, or you will need help from your parents. There are pros and cons to both.

3. Test Drive: Once you've found a car you like within your budget, make a test-drive appointment. Test a few different vehicles because every car will feel a bit different.

4. Solidify the Deal: Once you're clear about which car you like, it's time to talk numbers. Work with the sales agent to crunch the numbers and be absolutely certain you can afford it.

Understanding Insurance

Vehicle Insurance is a financial protection used when your car is damaged, stolen, or after an accident. Insurance covers the cost of medical bills if someone is hurt. And it will cover some, or all of the damages, depending on certain factors.

If you damage your car without an accident, you could be covered. For example, backing into a light pole or weather damage to the vehicle. Insurance also covers theft.

It's illegal to drive without insurance, so this is a non-negotiable.

Insurance works differently all over the World. In North America, insurance protection follows the car. So as long as a legal driver is driving an insured vehicle, coverage is valid.

In the UK, the insurance follows the driver, which means the driver can drive whichever vehicle they like, as long as they are insured.

This differs, but the main principles of insurance are the same. You choose the coverage. The insurance company determines the fault and whose insurance pays for the damage and then sends payment directly to you or to the mechanic shop.

Each policy is made up of various types of coverage. Depending on your needs, car, driving habits, and what you can afford, you can add different types of car insurance to a basic policy. I'll list out the main three here. Please refer to your local insurance provider for the most accurate information.

- **Liability/Third Party:** This is often the minimum coverage required to be on the road. This insurance protects you if you cause damage to another's property. This insurance also pays for any injuries caused.
- **Collision:** This covers the costs of repairing your vehicle damage, regardless of fault.
- **Comprehensive:** this protects your car when it's damaged by vandalism or theft, harsh weather, fire, and hitting an animal.

Insurance is different everywhere, so it can't be explained in one way only. However, there's always baseline protection for injury and damage for yourself and others on the road. Then you add on what feels best for you.

The Scene of a Crash

With driving comes risks. It's good to read these steps now, so you have a reference and know what to do if you have an accident.

Stay Calm: First of all, breathe. The calmer you are, the better you'll process.

Think Safety: If you can't get out of your car, turn on your hazard lights, call emergency services, and wait for help to arrive. If there are no injuries and you can still drive your vehicle, move to a safe spot that isn't blocking traffic.

Check for Injuries: See if anyone involved in the crash has any injuries. But not all injuries can be seen immediately. If you get out of the car to assess the damage and feel lightheaded or dizzy, call emergency services and sit down if you can.

Driver's Info Swap: Ask to see the driver's licenses of the other drivers involved and take down their license numbers. Confirm their name, address, phone number, insurance company, and policy number. Remember to write down their license plate number. Snapping photos of both the license and plates is a good idea.

Take Notes: If the crash is minor, take pictures and write the details down. Detailed notes and photos of the scene may help insurance decide who is at fault. Write a description of the vehicles involved (year, make, model, and color). Take photos (or draw a diagram) of the scene, including vehicles, road damage, and traffic signs. Make sure you write down the date, time, and weather conditions, as you could easily forget this later. If there are witnesses, see if you can get their names and contact info in case you need this.

Believe it or not, even if you think an accident was your fault, it might not be. There are particular rules of the road that insurance companies go by. Avoid placing (or accepting) blame or fault at the scene. If the crash is major, involve the police and take your direction from them.

File a Claim

Once you're settled and safe, contact your insurance company to inform them of the incident. A claim must be filed to use the insurance protection. They will get an account of what happened as accurately as possible.

You'll take your vehicle to a service garage specializing in insurance claims. Your vehicle will be evaluated and assessed by an insurance adjuster. Then, the insurance company will let you know the results and next steps.

Maintenance & Repair

I mentioned earlier that the car's original purchase might be the most affordable part of car ownership. There's no short-cutting this one - you must maintain your vehicle by servicing it regularly. It's a good idea to find and establish a relationship with a garage with a trustworthy mechanic, perhaps with the help of mom and dad, friends/parents of friends, or other people you know.

Learning basic vehicle repair techniques to fix an issue for yourself or someone you know is also valuable. But you don't *have* to know these skills to own a vehicle. You can invest in an auto club like CAA or AAA and access emergency assistance for flat tires, a dead battery, or a tow if you're involved in an accident, etc. Often these memberships offer auto insurance at a lower rate as well.

Let's go over some car maintenance practices.

Change a Flat Tire

Getting a flat can be frustrating and even scary, and remember you can ALWAYS call a professional in to help.

But if you're comfortable, knowing how to quickly put on a spare is hero-like. Most vehicles have a baby spare tucked away inconspicuously. Be sure to locate yours!

- Do your best to safely pull over if you pop a tire while driving.
- Turn on your hazard lights so you can be seen.
- Use a heavy wrench to loosen the lug nuts.
- Lift the car with the jack (most cars have these in hidden compartments also)
- Remove the lug nuts, then the tire.
- Put the baby spare tire on.
- Put the lug nuts back.
- Lower the car.
- Tighten the lug nuts as much as you can.
- Drive slowly to the nearest shop to get a full tire replacement.

Jump Start a Car

If you accidentally leave a dome light on overnight, your battery could be drained the following day, and you'd need to jump-start it.

- Park another car close to the dead one. Get your batteries as close as possible.
- Turn the cars off, pop the hoods and untangle your jumper cables.

- Attach the cable to the dead car **first**.
- Red clamp on the positive (+) terminal of the dead battery. Then red clamp to the working battery's positive (+) terminal.
- Clamp one black negative (-) cable to the <u>working battery's</u> negative side.
- **Don't connect it to the dead battery here.**
- In the dead vehicle, locate an unpainted metal surface connected to the frame and attach the black, negative (-) clamp.
- Start the working car. Start the dead car.
- Remove the cables in the reversed order you attached them.
- Let the car engine run for several minutes to charge the battery.

Check & Change the Oil

This seems basic but is vital to the functioning of your vehicle. You must check and periodically change the oil in your vehicle. Motor oil lubricates the engine. It protects all the moving parts and prevents them from rubbing against one another. Without oil, metal-on-metal would destroy your engine in a very short time.

Checking oil levels is straightforward while changing oil is a bit messier. You can opt to have the oil changed professionally, but you'll still need to check the levels in your car regularly.

- Before you turn on your engine, pop the hood and locate the dipstick.
- Pull this out entirely and wipe it clean with a rag or towel.
- Then put the dipstick all the way back in.
- Pull it out once more and check the oil level at the end. The dipstick will indicate where the level of oil should be at.
- If your oil is low, add the proper type of oil to the oil fill location.

- To change the oil, you'll need to be below the engine. It's best to elevate the vehicle. You can also opt for a towel on the ground, although you risk getting oil on yourself!
- Remove the drain plug and drain the oil into a container.
- Unscrew the oil filter and remove this, too (ensure you remove the rubber gasket!)
- Let the oil drain for a while, until you see a drip instead of a stream of oil.
- Put the new filter and drain plug in place and wipe any spilled oil.
- Pour in the new oil. Be sure you buy the proper oil for your vehicle.

Change the Battery

Car batteries age over time and will drain faster the more you drive. Another sign you might need to change the battery is if your car has trouble starting up, especially in cold temperatures. If you haven't turned your car on for a while, it's another reason your battery could be completely dead and won't hold a charge, even with a boost. Throw on some gloves, grab your new battery and let's go.

- Remove the terminal covers if there are any.
- Loosen, and disconnect the negative cables FIRST.
- Remove the clamp from the negative post.
- Disconnect the positive cables and clamp SECOND.
- Loosen the bolt that secures the battery and lift the battery out of the car (keep it upright).
- Replace the old battery with a new one.
- Put the cable clamps back.
- Have fun resetting your clock and radio presets!

Gassing Up

So you're driving your car for the first time without mom and dad. And you realize you've never added gas yourself!

Gulp! Here's how:

- Locate the small gas symbol on your dashboard. This is often near the area that indicates your speed. Next to it, you'll see an arrow pointing to the side of the car your tank is on. Sometimes the side is depicted by the handle of the gas symbol.
- Pull up and turn your car off.
- You need to prepay for fuel. You can use your debit/credit card or head inside to use cash.
- Choose the fuel grade. Most vehicles are fine with regular fuel, but if you have a luxury vehicle, add premium fuel to preserve the engine.
- Put the nozzle into the tank, and pull up the trigger to begin the gas flow. A sensor will detect when you're full and shut off automatically.
- Screw the gas cap back and shut the fuel door. Boom!

Kim's Corner: *In all Seriousness...*

Owning a car is pretty awesome, and I imagine most teens aspire to have their own wheels and feel the freedom it brings. And... with driving comes great responsibility too.

Driving is easy peasy on a nice day, on a quiet road with little traffic. However, driving can also be very dangerous, like on congested roads, at high speeds, or in bad weather. In some cases, a vehicle accident can cause permanent damage or even death.

As a driver, you must be cautious and consider many safety elements before getting behind the wheel.

Don't Drink and Drive: Your response time is significantly decreased when alcohol or drugs are consumed. Consider the implications of causing a bad accident when impaired. Just. Don't. Do It.

Don't Speed: Speeding is likely one of the most significant factors contributing to crashes. Speed limits are in place for the general safety of the public. Trust me, it's not worth the risks or the speeding tickets. You'll only get there a few minutes faster.

Forget the Phone: Seriously. Put your cell phone away. If you need to text, pull over. I realize there are wireless Bluetooth systems that let you talk on the phone while driving, BUT your brain cannot give 100% attention on the road if you're talking on the phone. Please just pull over if you need to chat.

Avoid Distractions: Don't mess around with the music, the temperature, or the seat while driving. Don't eat, and please don't put your makeup on, ladies! Just focus on the road, ask a passenger for help, or safely pull over to adjust what's needed.

Wear your Belt: You never know when or where an accident can occur. Even if traveling a short distance, wear your seatbelt.

Opt-Out of Bad Weather: If you don't have to drive in bad weather - don't. Stay indoors, or call a taxi if you have to go out.

Defensive Driving: I didn't say 'aggressive'! Defensive driving is actually the opposite. Stay calm, give lots of space from the vehicle ahead of you, drive slowly, yield to others… you get the point.

TEN

Personal Safety

Having basic first aid knowledge is essential. Even with such easy access to the internet, it's still a good idea to have a written manual for the basics. This section is about your personal safety, including physical and online safety.

Basic First-Aid

Basic first aid means providing primary medical care to someone injured or ill. More often, this means treating burns, cuts, or insect stings. It could also mean providing support to someone in the middle of a medical emergency.

If you experience a medical emergency, remember the **DRSABC** first aid method. You can remember this by thinking *'Doctors'* and *'ABC.'* It represents;

- **Danger**: Check for danger (for others around or the injured person). Be sure not to put yourself in harm's way when trying to assist someone else.

- **Response:** Check if the person is conscious. Do they respond to you talking, touching their hands, or squeezing their shoulder?
- **Send for Help:** Call your emergency number. That's 9-1-1 in the US and Canada. 0-0-0 in Australia, and 1-1-1 in New Zealand.
- **Airway:** Check if the person's airway is clear. If they're not responsive, open their mouth and look inside. If their mouth isn't clear, tilt the person to the side, open their mouth wide, and remove anything obstructing.
- **Breathing:** Check if they're breathing. Look at the chest for movements, put your ear near their mouth and nose to listen, or place your hand on the lower part of their chest. If they're unconscious yet breathing, turn them carefully to the side, ensuring you align their head, neck, and spine. Keep monitoring their breathing until help arrives.
- **CPR:** This stands for cardiopulmonary resuscitation. If an adult appears unconscious and is not breathing, lay them flat on their back. Place the heel of one hand toward the center of the person's chest and your second hand on top. Apply pressure firmly but smoothly 30 times. Tilt the person's head, lifting their chin to bring back their breathing. Pinch their nostrils, place your opened mouth firmly on top of their open mouth, and blow into it twice. Continue with 30 compressions and two breaths until trained help arrives or the individual responds. The CPR method for babies and children below eight is similar but with different techniques and repetitions. It's always a good idea to get formal CPR training.

Cuts & Scrapes

- **Wash your Hands:** This helps avoid infection.
- **Stop Bleeding:** Most minor cuts and scrapes will stop bleeding naturally. But where necessary, apply pressure

using a clean cloth or bandage. Elevate the area of the wound until the bleeding stops.

- **Clean It:** Rinse the cut under running water, and use soap to wash around it if you can. Avoid iodine or hydrogen peroxide, as this can cause irritation.
- **Apply Ointment:** Just a thin layer of petroleum jelly (vaseline) or antibiotic ointment can be applied next.
- **Cover:** Use a bandage or gauze with tape. But it's best to leave it uncovered if the wound is minor.
- **Change Dressing:** This can be done daily or when the bandage is dirty/wet.
- **Monitor:** Check for signs of infection; the skin around the wound for redness, increasing pain, swelling, warmth, or drainage. If there are signs of infection, please see a doctor.

Burns

Kitchen-related injuries from hot beverages, soups, and microwaved foods are common. But burns can also be caused by the sun, flames, chemicals, electricity, and steam. Major burns need emergency medical help, and minor burns can usually be treated with first aid.

Minor Burns:

- **Cool It:** Place the affected area under cool running water for about 10 minutes. If it's your face, apply a cool (not cold), wet cloth until the pain subsides. If it's your mouth (from a hot drink or food), put a small piece of ice in your mouth for a few minutes.
- **Clear the Area:** If you're wearing a ring or other tight items around the burned area, gently but quickly remove them before any swelling starts.
- **Leave Blisters:** Blisters protect the burn from infection, so don't break them. If a blister breaks on its own, use water to clean the area, then apply an antibiotic ointment.
- **Apply Lotion:** Once the burn is cooled, apply lotion that contains cocoa butter or aloe vera.

- **Bandage:** Wrap a clean bandage around the burn. Keep it loose to avoid placing too much pressure on the skin.
- **Pain Reliever:** If needed, take a pain reliever such as ibuprofen or acetaminophen.

Major Burns: Take the following steps until help arrives.

- **Protect:** For electrical burns, ensure the power source is turned off. If the person's clothing is stuck to the burn, don't attempt to remove them.
- **Clear the Area:** Remove jewelry, belts, and other tight items, as swelling can occur quickly.
- **Cover:** Loosely cover the burn with a clean cloth or gauze.
- **Elevate:** If possible, raise the burned area above heart level.
- **Monitor:** Watch for signs of shock (cool skin, shallow breathing, or weak pulse.)

Bites

Insect bites and stings can often be treated at home. Bites can cause swelling, itching, and stinging that goes away in a couple of days.

For mild reactions to insect bites or stings:

- Remove any stinger you can see.
- Wash the affected area gently with soap and water.
- For 10 to 20 minutes, lightly compress the sting or bite area with a cloth dampened with cold water.
- If the bite occurs on the leg or arm, raise it above heart level.
- Apply calamine lotion or baking soda to the affected area. Repeat several times daily till the symptoms go away.
- Take an oral anti-itch medicine (antihistamine) to reduce itchiness.
- If needed, take a non-prescription pain reliever.

Some bites or stings can transmit viruses, parasites, or disease-causing bacteria, and some stings may cause severe allergic reactions. If the swelling increases, you see signs of infection, or you're not feeling well, please seek medical care.

Sprains

Sprains are most common in your ankle. It happens when a joint gets stressed by overextending, which can cause a stretch or tear in your ligaments.

Symptoms vary depending on how severe the injury is. When the injury occurs, you may feel or hear a 'pop' sound within the joint.

This can be accompanied by pain, bruising, swelling, and joint restriction. If this happens, rest it, ice it, compress it and raise it up.

To prevent sprains, stretch regularly before and after strength training exercises.

Get a First Aid Kit

A first-aid kit in your home (and your car if you have one) lets you treat common injuries and emergencies. I recommend investing in 1 or 2. You can get these everywhere; your local grocery store, super-stores, or online.

Most kits will have the basics for minor injuries; bandages, wraps, gauze, ointments, gloves, scissors, disinfectants, tape, etc.

It's a good idea to know what's inside once you get your kit. And remember to restock after you use items.

When to See the Doc

Major symptoms and big incidents aren't the only reasons to see the doctor. The following list isn't exclusive of when to seek medical attention; it's a guide. You know your body better than anyone, so follow your instincts.

If you're concerned about something, that's a good enough reason to seek medical advice. And early detection can lead to better outcomes for many conditions.

Persistent High Fever

If your fever is over 103° Fahrenheit (39.4° Celsius) or lasts more than 3 days, call it in.

Cold Gets Bad

If your common cold takes a downward turn. Watch for severe coughing that lingers for two or more weeks, sustained congestion, flu-like symptoms, difficulty breathing, swallowing, pains in the chest, and excessive vomiting.

Chest, Stomach or Pelvic Pain

Abnormal or intense pain in these areas can indicate an underlying issue.

Unexplainable Weight Loss

This could signal health challenges. See your doctor if you've unintentionally lost over 10% of your body weight within the last six months.

Confusion

If you experience confusion accompanied by sleep challenges, feelings of anxiety, or depression, please seek medical attention.

Shortness of Breath

Unless you're at high altitudes, in extreme temperatures, or exercising, difficulty breathing should be checked by a doctor.

Concussion

If you had a significant fall or suffered a head blow, watch for concussion symptoms, like difficulty concentrating, headaches or irritability. If these develop, please seek help.

Emergency Preparedness

No one hopes for disasters, but they sometimes happen, depending on where in the World you live. It's challenging to be 100% prepared for every single emergency situation, but some basics can be considered.

- **Tune into Local Stations:** Local radio or TV stations will have the latest information on fire, storms, or anything heading your way. Find these stations in advance so you're not looking for them at the last moment.
- **Prep Stock:** Stockpile some nonperishable food, water, and medicine. Aim for about a week's worth. Stick with plastic bottles, fill them with water, and stock up on canned foods. Have nut butters and other long-lasting items. Ensure you have extra prescription medicine you might need.
- **Full First Aid Kit:** Make sure your first aid kit is always complete - remember to restock what you use and have the basics ready.
- **Avoid Tap Water:** During a natural disaster, tap water can become contaminated. Best to not use it if possible.
- **Keep Important Docs Safe:** Keep your passports, social security cards, birth certificates, etc., in a water/fireproof container. If these get lost, you could be in a worse situation.
- **Conserve Battery:** Keep your phone in battery-saver mode to preserve its life if you can't charge it.
- **Remember the Animals:** From domestic animals to farm animals. Be sure to have them tagged in case you get separated. And keep some extra food on hand for them too.

Online Safety

It's critical to understand the potential dangers of our ever-shifting online world. I'm not saying you should be scared - I'm suggesting the importance of being aware and taking the necessary precautions to be safe. Let's talk about some of these.

- **Use Solid Passwords:** When creating passwords, find the sweet spot between making them so easy anyone could figure them out and making them so hard that you can't remember them. You want strong and memorable passwords. Try these ideas:
- Use a combination of a phrase, shortcut codes, or acronyms that mean something significant to you. For example, **BeTaL8ThAnN3Va** (Better late than never) or **LTZm8k$2D** (Let's make money today).
- Let your passwords have common elements across specific sites. For example, **L0Gn_IN2_FB** (Logging into Facebook) or **L0Gn_IN2_YT** (Logging into YouTube)
- **Public Internet:** Many places, like airports, coffee shops, and restaurants, offer free internet with no passwords. While it's easy to connect to these, there are risks of being hacked from the public network. Your information and personal details could be compromised or exposed to malware, which is infected software that can corrupt your files and damage your system.
- **Get a VPN:** A Virtual Private Network connection is a good idea if you have to connect to public or unsecured connections. It gives an extra layer of security and privacy so you can browse freely and safely and hide your web activities and location.
- **Use SSL Connections:** Secure Sockets Layer is a security protocol that creates encryption between a web server and a web browser. This means you can still encrypt your communication without a VPN. Ensure the "Always Use HTTPS" option is selected for websites you use.
- **Turn Off Sharing:** When using a public internet connection, you likely have no need to share anything. So turn off sharing aspects of your computer like Bluetooth.

- **Keep Wi-Fi Off:** This prolongs your battery life, but more importantly, it keeps you secure. The Wi-Fi hardware on your computer always sends and receives data with networks within range. So if you don't need the internet, try switching your Wi-Fi off.

Dating Safety

In the age of swiping right or left, the World of dating has moved a lot to virtual avenues. If you're online dating, move slowly and get to know someone first before meeting them in person. Putting yourself out there too fast can make you an easy target and put you at risk.

If you're meeting a new person, there are some critical aspects to consider to keep yourself safe. And I totally get that safety precautions aren't top of mind when you're into someone. But it's so necessary to think about.

- **Protect your Digits:** Switching from virtual flirting to texting is common when there's a good connection. However, please take your time giving out your phone number. There's no taking it back! Once they have this, they could text, call, or even hack into your phone if they're super tech-savvy.
- **Meet Publicly:** Meet in public places you're familiar with for the first few dates. Try a park, restaurant, or coffee shop. Avoid meeting in dark, secluded areas, and stay away from remote places (like long hikes in the wilderness), as there may not be anyone around if you need help.
- **Trust Yourself:** If your instincts tell you something isn't right, listen! If you think someone lied to you, you're probably right.
- **Share:** Always tell a friend where you're going and with whom. Make sure someone knows what's happening and when you plan to be home. You can even check in with them during the date.

- **Gotta-Go Excuse:** It's 100% OK to leave a date early if the other person is making you uncomfortable. Have a plan in place before you go to tell them, 'you gotta go!'. I'm not saying to be rude here, but it's better to exit stage left than to put yourself in danger.
- **You CAN Ghost:** Sometimes, it's better to be super duper clear than to have someone be uncertain about your interest in them. Some people can take disinterest as a challenge and continue pursuing you. If you're really not interested, tell the person kindly, and it's OK not to respond to their calls and texts. This is a clear message.

Kim's Corner: *Online Photo Sharing*

The decisions you make now affect your life in the future. Nothing is closer to the truth than feeling regret about sharing specific photos of yourself online. I understand that when you're in a relationship with someone, at the time, it can feel great to share flirty, suggestive, or revealing photos. But before you do, consider the impacts.

What happens if you break up? What if the other person feels vengeful and wants to make you feel embarrassed or angry like they do? What if they share the photo with their friends? How would that make you feel?

In addition, when your picture is loaded online, it's there forever. Even if you delete a photo, it's stored somewhere on some super drive. Anyone clever enough can locate even deleted photos. Once it's up, it's up. And could be used against you in your life later.

The consequences of sharing provocative photos online could be detrimental. The risk is that you can't be sure whether your privacy will be respected.

In my opinion, it's just not worth it.

ELEVEN

Get The Gig

There are many benefits to getting a job, earning money being the most obvious. A summer or part-time job offers fundamental life skills like responsibility and commitment. And sets up essential foundations for your future.

I promise, getting a job isn't as scary as it might seem. Opportunities are swimming all around you, and being prepared changes everything.

What Kind of Work?

Typically, there are guidelines around safety standards, how many hours minors can work, and how much they get paid. But there are still lots of options for teens to work. Consider these ideas:

- Dog walker
- Kennel Assistant
- Dishwasher
- Server
- Camp Counselor
- House Cleaner

- Cashier
- Retail / Sales Associate
- Fast Food Attendant
- Library Assistant
- Warehouse Sorter
- Store Shelf Restocker
- Landscaper
- Brand Ambassador
- Barista
- Movie Theater Usher
- Concession Stand Worker
- Lifeguard
- Grocery Store Bagger
- Bloggers
- Golf Caddy
- Call Center Rep
- Personal Shopper

Types of Jobs

There are different types of jobs too, so consider which fits the most appropriately into your schedule.

- **Part-time:** Working less than 40 hours, and can be as little as 5 hours per week. Pay attention to how many hours the position is listed for.
- **Contract:** You're employed for a short-term basis, such as 1 month or 10 weeks.
- **Seasonal:** Some companies hire temporarily during a specific season, like a ski resort or summer camp.
- **Internship:** An initial position for a career. Some internships might pay you, while others offer school credit.
- **Entrepreneurship:** When you start your own business. If this is your thing, you can head to Kim's Corner at the end of this chapter for more info.

- **Volunteer:** Volunteering is a wonderful opportunity to gain job experience, build your network and learn new skills while supporting a cause you believe in.

How to Get a Job

Finding a first job as a teen can feel tricky. You can do this! Just go step by step, and you'll be working in no time!

- **Determine What you Want:** Think about how much you want to work, the skills you'd like to develop, your interests, and the type of environment you'd like to work in.
- **Search for Openings:** It's a global village out there. Jobs can be found on online job boards, newspapers, local shops, and company websites.
- **Align with your Interests:** Try to find a job you will like. For example, look for babysitting jobs if you enjoy caring for youngsters or lawn care companies if you enjoy being outside.
- **Get a Work Permit:** If you're under 16, you may need a work permit. These requirements will vary based on location, age, and industry, so find out what's required in your area.
- **Ask for References:** Ask coaches, teachers, and possible group leaders who understand your work ethic to be a reference for you.
- **Build a Network:** Ask your network if they know of any openings you might like. Word-of-mouth and referrals really go a long way!
- **Create your Resume:** I'll run you through how to write a resume in a jiffy!
- **Add a Cover Letter:** This explains your qualifications in greater detail and gives you the opportunity to articulate *why* you're interested in a particular position.

- **Apply:** Try and submit 10 - 15 applications a week. This will increase your chances of hearing back and keep your options open.
- **Follow Up:** Always check back about 2 weeks post application. This demonstrates your interest and professionalism.
- **Prepare for Interview:** You'll want to prepare ahead of time. See the section below.

Write a Resume

Making a good first impression on potential employers is essential. Ensure your resume is well organized and includes details of your most relevant skills (rather than a giant mash-up of everything). Read the job description you're applying for carefully so you can tailor your resume to fit that job.

If this is your FIRST resume and you lack work experience, you can still write a great resume. You can pull many templates online, so grab the one you like but keep it simple. Let's briefly go through the resume sections:

1. Contact Info

Make your contact details prominent, so it's one of the first things people see when they look at your resume. Put your name and contact information in a larger font than the rest of the resume.

- Name: First and last
- Phone Number: List just one.
- Professional Email: Use your name to register a professional email address, like john.smith@gmail.com
- Social Media: Pick one or two platforms that show you're best for the job. (Don't bother if you only share memes and selfies, though.)
- Website: If you have a portfolio or write for a blog that shows you can do the position, add it! That's gold on your resume!

There's no need to include personal information like your age that's not relevant to the job.

2. Objective

Your goals and long-term plans for your career are outlined in your resume's objective. Use two or three sentences to summarize who you are and attract attention. Focus on what you can do for *them* rather than on *yourself*.

Excited server applicant with no experience yet, but very willing to learn and work really hard. It'd be great to hire me so I can get experience.

Hard-working student looking to use amazing social skills to support dining excellence at Jerry's Diner. Passionate home cook. Eagle Scout. Medallion Lifeguard.

3. Education

Your education is your best asset when you have no work related-experience to showcase.

- School Name: Don't use slang. Copy the name from the school website or Google Maps.

- Graduation Date: If you still need to finish school, add an expected graduation date.
- Key Achievements: List awards or other achievements here.
- Extracurricular Activities: volunteering, organizing school events, being the president of a school club—these all show character!
- Favorite Classes: This shows a bit more of who you are, especially if the course is related to the position.
- GPA: Add your scores only if it's impressive. If not, feel free to cut it.

4. Work Experience

"But Kim, I don't HAVE any experience!"

I get it. You're writing a teen resume! You can showcase other experiences which are non work-related! Here are some ideas:

- Volunteer Work: List valuable experiences you've had volunteering.
- Freelancing Experience: These are odd babysitting gigs, helping your mom out in their office or mowing a neighbor's lawn, etc.
- Job Shadowing: A friend showed you how to use Photoshop, or you spent time with your dad at work. List it!
- Extracurricular Activities: Are you into sports? In a drama club? Book club? Play music?
- Personal Projects: Maybe you created an Instagram account for a school team, designed posters for a parade, or organized a talent show… list projects you've accomplished or been a part of.

5. Skills

Take a good look at the job description you're applying for and highlight the words that refer to the skills they might want. Then…

- List your Hard Skills: These are knowledge or abilities needed for the position, often gained through training, education, or other experiences (i.e., computer, management, or language skills, certifications, etc.).
- List your Soft Skills: These are personal attributes that would help you be successful in the position (teamwork, patience, good communication, etc.).
- Cross Reference: Compare your own skills with the job requirements.
- Make your List: Create a list of 5–8 skills relevant to the job you're applying for and add them to your resume.

6. Extras

This is where you'd list your past accomplishments, awards, honors, etc. It helps showcase you're an achiever, so don't be shy!

- Honors and Awards: Feel free to brag on your resume and list as many as possible.
- Activities: Describe things you do that are related to the position. For example, if you're applying for a dishwasher job, mention how you effectively help with chores at home.
- Associations: If you belong to any online or offline discussion groups, you could add those here.
- Certifications: Many certifications can be learned online, and some don't even cost anything.
- Interests and Hobbies: Add some of your interests, if applicable.
- Publications: Did your restaurant review get listed in the local paper? Or did your blog post get featured somewhere? Listing publications can be a great way to find a writing job.

Resume Tips

The goal of a good resume is to display yourself as the best person for the desired position. Once the main structure of your resume has been written, there's still a little more to do...

- **Stay Relevant:** Include only information and sections that make sense. Craft your resume for the role you're applying for.
- **Readable:** Keep your resume eye-friendly and include some space, but not too much space, or it will look empty.
- **Order:** List everything in reverse chronological order (meaning put your most recent listing at the top).
- **Use Figures:** Use numbers to quantify details where it makes you look good! Like listing your exact GPA, hours volunteered, the number of months you've achieved awards, etc.
- **Proofread:** After writing your resume, read it carefully to catch spelling or grammar errors. Ask a teacher, counselor, parent, or mentor to read your resume and give feedback.

Prep for the Interview

Many teens are interested in summer, part-time, and campus jobs. You'll want to stand out to get hired. And an interview is the perfect chance to impress a hiring manager. Here are some steps to help you rock your interview:

1. Research: Dig a little into the company you're interviewing with. Read the "About" section on their site, look into their social media pages, and read some of their reviews to see what others say about them. Get a feel for the company culture. Recruiters want to know how well you'll fit in. Bring knowledge of the organization to impress them.

2. Understand the Job: In your excitement of landing an interview, you may not remember the job description, especially if you applied to multiple companies. Read (and re-read) the job description to understand the required tasks and ask questions about those tasks..

3. Common Questions: There are standard interview questions asked in most interviews. The good news is you can go through some of these, prepare answers ahead of time and be ready when asked. See the following examples:

- *Why do you want the position?*
- *What do you know about the company?*
- *Why are you the best candidate for this role?*
- *What are some of your strengths and weaknesses?*
- *What's an accomplishment you feel proud of?*
- *What's your availability?*
- *Do you have any questions about the position?*

4. Prepare Stories: Storytelling is one way to stand out! Be ready to use real-life stories to respond to the likely phrase:

Tell me about a time when…

- *… you made a mistake.*
- *… had a disagreement with an adult.*
- *… had to lead something.*
- *… overcame a challenge.*
- *… witnessed something you knew was wrong.*
- *… worked on a team.*

5. Practice: Set up a mock interview with a trusted adult to practice your answers and role-play. Go a step further and dress up, bring copies of your resume and shake their hand. This will ease the nerves you may have for the real deal.

6. Dress the Part: This will be different based on the position, but you want to dress appropriately for the work you're applying for. Go one step above the casual outfits you wear to school, but maybe don't sport the full suit if you're applying to a restaurant position.

7. Manage Nerves: You might be nervous or anxious about your interview, especially if it's your first time! That's perfectly normal! You can anticipate your reactions (sweaty palms, shaky voice…) so they don't surprise you when you're in the interview. Acknowledgment helps to release some of the stress.

8. Thank You Note: Follow up with a short, personal note to your interviewer a few days after your interview. This can be handwritten, an email, or by phone. It's polite and reminds the recruiter you're extra keen.

9. Feedback: If you don't end up getting the position, consider asking if they have any feedback so you can do better next time. Don't be discouraged! This feedback supports you with valuable insights for the next one!

What to Wear

First impressions are vital in an interview. Before you even open your mouth to say anything, you speak volumes about yourself by your attire. And trust me, the manager is noticing! Here are a few tips to note:

- **Be Intentional:** Take some time to consider what's appropriate to wear for your interview. The "right" attire will vary based on industry, but you'll likely have an idea of what makes you look nice. Try on outfits until you find the perfect one that makes you feel confident and sharp. Put it aside and keep it clean until the big day!
- **Dress Code:** Some organizations are more casual, whereas others require more formal clothing. If you know people in the industry, ask them what they'd wear to an interview. But generally, do your best to choose clothes that give you a simple, clean look.
- **Power Outfit:** It's a good idea to invest in a few nicer clothes for interviews. Even if the company has a casual approach to clothing, you may still be expected to dress up

a little for the interview. It might cost you a little upfront, but landing a great job is worth it!

- **Appropriate Footwear:** Wearing dirty shoes with a smart outfit is a total no-no! I promise, your shoes DO get noticed. Wear footwear that matches your outfit, but don't sacrifice comfort entirely. You want to be relaxed for your line of questioning.
- **Forget the Flash:** Don't go overboard with bling! Accessories can be great for an outfit, but too much can be distracting. A nice belt and watch are excellent options for a Gent. Earrings and a necklace for a Lady are enough.

Besides your outfit, ensure your hair and fingernails are clean for your interview. And you're good to go! Good luck!

Kim's Corner: *How do I become an Entrepreneur?*

Depending on your background (and extra time), you might be encouraged to make money through your own means. I encourage you to dabble a little here if you feel inspired. Being an entrepreneur is an empowering journey that builds character that can take you far.

Want to give it a go?

#1) Determine the Service you'll Offer.

The main thing in business is that you must offer VALUE in exchange for a monetary reward. So how can you do that? The possibilities are endless. What do you love? What are you good at? Here are some ideas.

- Dog Walking
- Babysitting
- Tutoring
- House-cleaner
- Car Washing
- House-Sitting

- Errand-Running
- Lawn Mowing
- Blogging
- Survey Taking
- Freelance work (photography, writing)

#2) Build Knowledge

What can you learn to make your services stellar? Is there a babysitting course you can take? Are there online videos you can watch to improve your lawn-mowing skills?

#3) Start-Up Costs

In most cases, you don't need a ton of money to get going, but you MAY need to pick up supplies. If you don't have any money, you need to get creative or ask your parents for support. Map out the minimums you need and bring a solid plan for using the money.

#4) Set Pricing

Decide on a simple pricing structure for your services and how you'll accept payment.

#5) Network

The best bet, in the beginning, is to talk to people. Let your neighbors know you can shovel their snow this year or walk their dogs if they travel. Ask your parents to let their friends know you're ready to babysit. Word of mouth is extremely powerful, so leverage your networks.

#6) Keep Going

Not all businesses are successful overnight; it can take time, so don't be discouraged. You'll also have many distractions that could take you away from the business. Do your best to spend some time weekly building your new idea, talking to people, and thinking about how you can add value to other people's lives.

TWELVE

Be Successful

No collection of Life Skills would be complete without speaking about the following skills which support you in becoming a successful individual. When you work on these skills, you'll do well in any area of life.

They aren't necessarily *'learn them once'* kind of competencies. As long as you intentionally pursue them as you navigate the World, they'll become lifelong habits that will take you places!

Be Organized

Organization is a skill you want to develop because it'll help you manage demanding schedules in school, meet deadlines, and maintain extra-curricular activities. Not to mention, lots can go missing in your locker when things aren't systematized.

Being organized will pay off in all your years, so try these:

- **Use a Planner:** There's always a lot to do. You may have classes, the gym, home chores, community responsibilities, grocery shopping, and so on. It's easy for things to fall through the cracks. Grab yourself a physical planner. Or download an online app. Train yourself to write down what you need to do and by when.

- **Get a Good Backpack:** Use a multi-compartment backpack to stay super organized and know where everything is! Find one with at least 2 large areas for books, binders, or personal items. And zippered smaller pockets for smaller school supplies.
- **Try Color-Coding:** You could assign a color to each class in your binder or use different colored bags or bins to store various items.
- **Use Props:** Grab some sticky notes and keep them handy. They're great for making notes as you study textbooks. Buy erasers if you prefer to write with pencils and 'white-out' if you like ink. This keeps your pages clean if you need a correction. Use desk supply organizers at home and invest in a locker organizer for school.

Set Goals

Your ability to set goals you can achieve is a cultivated skill. The best technique for effective goal setting I've learned to follow is an acronym called **SMARTER**. When you create a goal, test them against seven yardsticks.

Specific: You need to clarify the priority points. Otherwise, there's no focus, and it makes *succeeding* uncertain. For example, if you say, "today, I will tidy up," that's not a specific goal because even if all you did was dust a few cobwebs, well, you *did* tidy up, didn't you?

Measurable: This lets you track your goals and ensure progress is happening. The metrics used will depend on the situation. For example, you could make a detailed list of all the specific parts of your room you need to clean. These measurable stats can also be numeric, as in studying for 1 hour, 4 nights per week.

Achievable: Is the goal realistic? Can it be achieved based on your abilities? What about within the time allotted? Can it be achieved at all? Look at this one as objectively as possible.

Relevant: This one is more big-picture. *Why* are you setting the goal? Your goal should align with your core values and be relevant to your desired life. If your values contradict your goal, it'll be challenging to achieve. For example, if your core value is freedom, then setting goals that have you on a rigid schedule won't support that.

Time-Based: Every goal must be based on time. Having a deadline creates urgency, but there's a sweet spot here. Deadlines can't be too soon, or they could be unrealistic. And if you base the timeline too far out, it's not a priority. For example, "I'll clean my room by 10am on Saturday" is a better goal than "I'll clean my room."

Evaluate: This step is about determining what's working and what can be done differently. If you evaluate your goals regularly, you'll be able to adjust aspects along the journey. And if you revisit your goal often, you'll stay motivated! Set up a system to remind yourself to evaluate how it's going.

Readjust: Revisions to your goal are often needed once you evaluate. How can better results be reached? Are there different metrics to track more effectively? An airplane is constantly monitoring and readjusting its flight path to reach its destination. You can do the same with your goals. You may have to try different approaches until you get closer to your goal.

Develop Discipline

Self-discipline is the ability to control your feelings and overcome challenges.

This means pushing yourself to do things that need to be done, sticking to goals you've set, and pursuing activities despite distractions.

There are many names for this: self-discipline, self-control, willpower… However you name it, these qualities set the achievers apart from the rest. Not only does this skill enable you to reach your goals, but you can also overcome many of life's challenges using discipline.

The benefits of developing self-discipline are enormous. Let's break it down to get you started:

- **Be Introspective:** Look inward to identify (and accept) your strengths and challenges. Self-awareness is a crucial step to self-discipline. When you're aware of the challenge, you can work toward overcoming it with dedication and discipline.
- **Post It:** Write your goal out and post it in a place you'll see it often. Try above your desk in your room, the bathroom mirror, the refrigerator, and inside your locker.
- **Think Why:** It's easy to forget about goals. Remind yourself *why* you even want what you want. Give yourself a reason for pushing onward.
- **Prioritize:** There's only so much you can do in a day, week, month, and year. Consider what's the most important and what can wait. If you have a big test to study for, do that before completing the smaller homework assignments.
- **Reward:** A little incentive can go a long way. It's OK to promise yourself a reward when you complete the goal you're reaching for.
- **Sleep:** It seems mundane but is very powerful. Sleep is a key factor in having a good mood, which helps you stay motivated and disciplined. Try creating a regular sleep routine or try soothing music to support good rest.
- **Say No:** It's easy to take too much on. Consider what's being asked of you, and only commit to what you can manage. You want to limit your 'discipline powers' so you can accomplish your goals and feel successful.
- **Tolerate Discomfort:** Pushing forward 'in spite of' can sometimes feel uncomfortable. See if you can accept and

even embrace these feelings, and just keep moving. You'll accomplish what you never thought possible by stepping out of your comfort zone and undoubtedly reach your goal.

- **Visualize:** When you focus on the desired outcome and *how you'll feel* once you attain success, you'll stay motivated.

Manage Your Time

Time management is an important skill to develop. With social media and other distractions on our cell phones, successful time management is harder than ever. However, use these tips, and you're well on your way!

Weekly Plan: Write out what you need to do for the week, month, or school year.

Monday	Tuesday	Wednesday	Thursday	Friday
21 Nov	22 Nov	23 Nov	24 Nov	25 Nov
	Math test			Soccer Practice

Add to Calendar: Use a physical planner or online software like google calendar. Place your event on the date it's needed.

Break it Down: If the main event includes smaller tasks, like studying. What's required to accomplish the task? How often do you need to study, and for how long?

Plot it: Work backward from the main event and add the smaller tasks to support the larger goal.

Monday	Tuesday	Wednesday	Thursday	Friday
14 Nov	15 Nov	16 Nov	17 Nov	18 Nov
	Study for Math Test			

Make a To-Do List: Look ahead for at least a week to see what's upcoming. If you have new events coming up, write them down. Then separate the list into 3 categories:

- Needs to get done (right away)
- Would like to get done (can wait)
- Want to do (in your free time)

TO DO LIST

Need to	Would like to	Want to
Biology home work	Research post-secondary	Hang with friends
Work on essay	Write resume	Watch a movie
Clean room		

Set Reminders: Set notifications for all your tasks from your phone so you'll be nudged no matter where you are. You can also jot down reminders in your physical planner.

Identify Productive Time: We each have a time of day when we get a lot done. It may be in the morning or right after school. When do you feel excited to get things done? When are your ideas and thinking super clear? Schedule tasks during this time.

Create Routine: This is very powerful. Even on a rough day, you can decrease stress by returning to structure. Routines help the brain create patterns and predictability; you won't waste time thinking about what's next.

Plan Free Time: All work and no play won't produce a balanced lifestyle. Be sure to include fun activities and downtime in your schedule.

Make Sound Decisions

Life is filled with choices. Some are easy, like what to have for breakfast, and others are more impactful, like choosing a career. Rational and intelligent decision skills are critical, especially if you feel unsure about something.

Rather than procrastinating, try the following to help you move forward.

- **Be calm:** It's easy to feel anxious about a tough decision. With stress, if you decide too quickly, your choice may be emotionally based rather than well thought out. Try taking a walk to relax your mind. Manage your stress so you can consider perspectives with a clear mind.
- **Take your Time:** Every choice has a consequence. So if you're making important decisions quickly, you'll need to be OK with the outcome. If you can, try not to make big decisions on a dime. Instead, create the time to contemplate your options, and consider the decision properly.
- **Weigh Pros & Cons:** Every decision has advantages and disadvantages. Before committing to a side, list the pros and cons and compare them. You can even take it one step further and write down the consequences of each.

- **Honor Values:** It's noteworthy to be true to yourself and make decisions that align with your values.
- **Seek Advice:** Ask people you trust, like your parents, teachers, coaches, or friends, what they think. Especially if your decision is one they've had to make and can relate to.
- **No Mistakes:** The point of analysis is to come to a conclusion. There's no right or wrong amount of time for assessing, but don't spend so much time in a quandary that you get stuck in a loop. Consider your options, and make a calculated call. If it's not the right move, you can correct and continue in most cases. Whatever you decide to pursue, there's always something to learn.

Solve Problems

You literally solve problems every day in tons of ways, but you may not be aware you're doing it. These skills are highly valued in personal and professional situations. And yet - we're not necessarily conscious of the skill.

If you encounter a challenge, shift your thinking about it as a problem. There's always a solution, so let's learn how to find that using a simple process, so you can be a natural problem solver.

What's the Challenge?

You'd be surprised how often we think we know the problem when we don't. Get everyone involved and put words to the actual issue. This will make the challenge solvable!

Why is it a Challenge?

Ask yourself some reflection questions like; What's causing the problem, and where did it come from? What's upsetting about this? Why do you need this to be different? Try and listen to how you feel about these. This reflection gives you insight into how you can shift this.

. . .

Ponder Possibilities

Brainstorm a list of all possible ways you could solve the challenge. Even if you're not sure you can pull it off, list it. Write down as many solutions as you can think of, even if they're totally out there! The point is to train your brain to consider options.

Assess the Best

Rate your solutions from 1 - 10 based on the pros and cons of each possibility. The solution you choose should directly solve the problem, so check back to the initial problem to be sure.

Get Going

Once a solution has been decided, plan it out. Consider who's involved and how. Ensure everyone who needs to be involved is fully enrolled in your initiative to solve the problem.

Check In

Part of effective problem-solving is adapting if things don't go as you'd expected. You may need to try a different solution if the challenge still exists. Go back to the first question in this process and reconsider. You may have a better understanding of what the issue is and can think of another solution.

Ethics & Integrity

Ethics are your core values and moral principles that govern your behavior. Like a list of rules you live by.

Integrity is how firmly you live your life according to those values and principles.

The truth is, we can't live our lives only considering what others need or like about us. As you go through your teens, you'll realize how you feel about many life experiences. You'll develop opinions and frustrations. You'll feel powerful in some areas and powerless in others. These concepts will naturally strengthen over time.

In short, people with strong ethics and high integrity tell the truth and are sincere. They take responsibility for their actions, treat others fairly, and behave consistently. You can probably sum this up with the saying, 'do the right thing, even when no one's looking.'

Every individual should strive to live this kind of life. Being true to your values, what you believe in, and how you stick to those beliefs will develop character and strength.

Kim's Corner: *There's no such thing as failure.*

Failure is often seen as something negative, but it's an integral part of life. Surprisingly, there's more to learn from *not succeeding* than succeeding! And it's the most successful people who have failed the most! (Ponder that one for a moment.)

I can imagine the pressure and anxiety teens could feel around achieving everything they set out to do. The list is long... Perhaps to meet parents' expectations, look good on social media, get noticed by their crush, do well on the sports team, get into a good school, or get a good job.

But when their identity is still forming during these precious years, even small failures can lead to heartbreak, depression, negative self-talk, and giving up hope. In addition, our society tends to celebrate success rather than highlight the *journey* toward success, including the setbacks and failures.

Just as a baby falls many times while learning to walk, expect failures when you strive toward new heights. **Failure is a stepping stone, not a block, to success.**

Failing has many benefits and is FULL of growth opportunities. We develop meaning from painful situations which make our lives richer. Not succeeding also gives us first-hand knowledge to over-come the challenge!

Being unsuccessful also helps us appreciate and value what's on the other side - success! And when you work toward a goal, experience failure, and keep on going, you're building perseverance, which helps you achieve your long-term goals.

When it comes to failing, cultivate a growth mindset, and use the experience as a tool. The key is how to react when failure shows up. Please don't listen to people who try to rub it in. Or who say, 'I told you so.' Ignore the negativity and focus on what you learned to leverage the failure.

It's really OK to fail - just don't give up! Setbacks are perfectly normal. See what you can do differently next time, regroup, keep your chin up, and keep moving.

THIRTEEN

Rockin' Relationships

As a teenager, I struggled to decide what direction to go in post-secondary school and what program to study. My mom's advice has stuck with me all these years.

She said, "Kimberly, I know this seems like a really big decision - and it is. I want you to understand that although what you decide to study is important, it's not everything about your success in life. The *relationships* you develop with others will take you significantly farther. You could have the highest grades and ace all your studies. But you won't be happy if you can't create harmonious relationships within your interactions. Whatever direction you pursue, cultivate good relationships, and you'll do well."

Such great advice!

Having excellent relational skills is a significant factor in success. Even if someone is incredibly brilliant and talented, if they walk all over others or treat people with no respect on their journey, they won't thrive for very long.

Why? Because our opportunities, information, and knowledge come from other people. Cultivating and maintaining positive relationships is the cornerstone to receiving what we need to be happy and prosperous.

I'm referring to more than just romantic relationships. It's friendships and family relationships too. I'm also referring to relationships you foster with your teachers, coaches, neighbors, baristas, sales associates, and even the mailman.

Anyone you regularly interact with is considered a relationship. Let's talk about a few things you can implement right away to work on developing this underrated skill.

Practice Politeness

These days, there seems to be a more casual way of communicating than when I grew up. Which is fine. However, sometimes that causal-ness can be portrayed as 'I don't care' or even come off as rudeness.

Fundamentally, everyone wants to feel respected and loved. When we're polite, we offer others this kindness and consideration.

In addition, being polite also implies humility rather than entitlement. And in a world of rapid first impressions, we have mere moments to make lasting impressions on others.

It's essential to be well-mannered. But what does that mean anyhow?

- **Golden Words:** Use "Please" and "Thank you" all the time where it's appropriate.
- **Apologize:** When you realize you're wrong, acknowledge and take responsibility quickly.
- **Don't Interrupt:** When someone is speaking, give them space and let them land on their point before you provide a rebuttal. It might be tempting to jump in and assert your thoughts, but interrupting isn't kind. Wait until someone's complete, then share your thoughts.

- **Eye Contact:** Look at people directly when you're speaking to them. It speaks about your confidence and communicates respect. But don't stare or glare! The idea is to maintain eye contact for about 5 seconds at a time. Practice it with mom and dad and let them give you feedback.
- **Shake Hands:** Go ahead and shake when it's appropriate. It's a form of respect.
- **Healthy Respect:** If you have to sneeze or cough while with others, do so into your elbow or a tissue and remember to say, "excuse me."

Use Names

A person's name is the most significant connection to their identity and individuality.

Using someone's name when speaking to them gives you a better *connection a*nd makes them feel valued and respected.

It's a good idea to find out how they like to be addressed. Maybe they have a shorter name they prefer. Or perhaps the individual you're speaking to favors formalities and wants to be called Mr or Mrs. Last Name. Remembering someone's name and using it when you see them again will make a person feel significant.

Remember, this is a skill, so you'll improve with practice. Try to use a person's name every time you see them. Saying their name, as well as *hearing* the name, helps to solidify the memory.

It's also perfectly acceptable to ask someone how they pronounce their name if you're unsure. In fact, I'd imagine this would be a sign of respect because you're indicating it matters to use their *correct* name.

Use people's names wherever you can, when speaking to them, by text, email, and other social media messages to develop and maintain a positive relationship with someone.

Reciprocal Convo's

Conversations are the most beautiful ways to build relationships. That person you call your best friend is only so because you have the best conversations with them. Just as it's important to feel heard when you're speaking, it's also important to listen to others. One way of indicating this is through reciprocal conversation.

This includes multiple exchanges of asking and answering questions and then building on each other's comments. This process involves awareness, listening carefully, and knowing what to say next.

Listening attentively and engaging with what someone has said is an essential skill that conveys politeness and strengthens emotional bonds. These conversation skills also help to build confidence and sustain meaningful friendships.

To do this, you and another individual talk about a specific topic and go back and forth, each responding or adding to the other person's comment. It's imperative to **listen** while the other person is speaking. Wait your turn, and don't talk over them. The topic of conversation gets tossed back and forth a few times until it naturally moves on.

Remember to listen with interest. It's easy to *look* like you're listening when you're really preparing what to say next. But effective communication requires paying attention to what someone says and THEN forming a response.

If you're speaking to someone in person, notice their body language too. This gives significant clues into their thinking and how you might respond.

Here are a few ways to support Reciprocal Conversations:

- **Ask Questions:** When questions are related and appropriate, they're a lovely way to keep a conversation flowing. It shows you're interested in what the other person's saying and makes them feel valued.

- **Include Follow-Ups:** Asking follow-up questions is a great way to let your listener know you're genuinely paying attention. These questions begin with Who, What, Where, When, Why, and How.
- **More Details:** Asking for more information can also be a great way to keep the conversation going.
- **Stay Engaged:** Do your very best not to yawn or glaze over while someone speaks to you, as it communicates disrespect.

Listen... Really!

Listening skills are essential to effective communication and a key element of happy relationships. When you listen intently to someone, you will improve your relationship with them.

Our own minds are very quick. We're always thinking, considering, or judging. Even when we *think* we're not thinking, we are! It takes deliberate consciousness to *not think.* And here's the punch line. To listen, and I mean **really listen,** you can't be thinking.

But not to worry! You'll spend a lifetime learning and developing this skill.

Some tips around politeness have already been shared, but try these additional tips to help:

- **Limit Judgements:** When you're listening, try not to criticize the speaker in your mind. Avoid being negative or judgmental because this compromises your ability to listen.
- **Be Open:** Listen with an open mind. The speaker is giving you their perspective only. By letting the person share and show up however they do, you're offering the respect of letting them be who they are.
- **Wait for the Pause:** Even if you need more clarification on what someone is saying, let them complete their thought before you ask for clarity. If you let them finish, you may understand what you were missing.

- **Empathize:** This means considering the other person's feelings. Consider what it would be like if *you* were in *their* situation. You could also try mirroring what someone you're speaking to is displaying. If they're sad, your facial expression, words, and body language could also convey similar emotions in support.
- **Send Signals:** As you're listening, you can send verbal and non-verbal communication back, so they know you're actively listening. You could say, "wow, that's amazing news!" nod your head and use appropriate facial expressions.
- **Take Notes:** If you're receiving instructions, taking notes is an active way to show you're listening. You can also repeat the task, so they know you understand what to do.

Politely Say 'NO'

Saying NO can be a tricky thing to do! We all want to be great friends, students, employees, partners, and many other things. A common characteristic is taking too much on, which can cause other parts of life to suffer.

In general, saying YES to opportunities is great! And saying NO when you're maxed (or simply aren't feeling something) is perfectly acceptable. There's absolutely nothing wrong with having respectable boundaries; it's a dance between giving and receiving.

Learning to express no-thanks will leave you much more satisfied and without the resentment that can drag into a relationship when we do things we don't *really* want to.

If it's too hard to say NO, how about 'Let me get back to you'? Sometimes giving yourself the space to process the request is all you need. It's also easier to decline when you're clear about why you can't help.

If you anticipate being asked something you can't or don't want to do, you could rehearse your NO! Role-play in front of the mirror or with someone you trust.

It's important to understand, in most cases, you are NOT required to explain your decision. Offering an excuse may seem like the polite way to decline, but it can sometimes make things worse. Be polite and appreciative, but you truly don't owe an explanation to anyone.

How about some concrete phrases to decline and grow your NO-muscle;

I'm honored, but I can't...

Unfortunately, it's not a good time...

Darn! I'm not able to fit this in...

Sadly, I have something else...

No, thank you! It sounds amazing, so maybe next time...

I'm not taking on anything else right now...

Thank you so much, but I can't...

Sorry, I have another commitment...

Be Coachable

Being coachable is the willingness to accept feedback and the ability to use this feedback for improvement. It's not shrinking when someone *(kindly)* asks to see a change from you, especially if it's necessary to succeed.

If you're coachable, you'll accept what someone is saying about you or your performance and use that feedback to become better, whether that's a better athlete, student, music player, friend, partner, or other.

If you can hear what someone is saying THROUGH what might sound like criticism, and then USE it to your advantage - holy-moly, you'll fly toward any success path you choose!

What can you actually DO to become coachable? Try these:

- **Stay Positive:** If you choose it, this feedback is an opportunity to improve yourself. Try and look at it from the perspective that this actually benefits you. Plus, if you have a positive attitude about someone's feedback, they're more likely to give you more detailed feedback.
- **Don't Justify:** It's tempting to justify your behavior when receiving feedback. Consider the perspective that the other person is trying to help you by offering their comments. Do your best to prioritize improvement over being 'right.'
- **Ask for It:** What if you made a conscious effort to ask for feedback rather than waiting for it? Looking for and asking for feedback shows you're highly coachable.
- **Question It:** Once you've received your observations from someone, you can ask them questions or request more clarity on how they see you improving.
- **Say Thanks:** When you receive feedback from a coach, teacher, or parent, try to respond graciously with "thank you." Being appreciative indicates you're willing to take their comments into consideration.
- **Reflect:** Think about the feedback you've received and how you can use it to change your behavior and make personal improvements.
- **Make the Change:** What action steps can you take to change your behavior? Consider writing down the desired behavior and create a plan on how to effectively improve the behavior.

Kim's Corner: *Curiosity is a Sweet Spot in Life!*

Albert Einstein said, "I have no special talents. I am only passionately curious."

When we are curious, our minds remain open to consider available possibilities. **This is a major SuperPower you want to harness.**

There's always a dynamic between people, and it can be challenging to receive feedback. As in, it might be harder to hear a brother or sister tell you how to study better. The same advice may be better received through a teacher or parent. But the actual advice might still be beneficial.

And if we're defensive or feel shame when hearing feedback, it's easy to shut down. Once again, denying the potential for possibility.

Being curious is the life hack here. Get interested in how you might be coming across, and keep an open mind. This cuts through emotions that may block your potential, so you can benefit from what is said.

Being curious supercharges learning, breaks bad habits, and will let you live a happier, more fulfilled life.

FOURTEEN

Ride The Emotional Wave

There isn't a more accurate way of describing the teen years than calling it an 'emotional wave.' Not only is there a TON of learning (on everything in this book and more!), but physiological changes are also occurring. This includes hormones kicking in, which literally change how your brain works and can really affect your day-to-day life.

It's no secret there are plenty of sources for a teen to feel big emotions, with demands from school, family dynamics, managing a social life, balancing extracurricular activities, and navigating puberty, to name a small handful.

These years are a volatile time when it comes to emotions. But I promise you're not alone, even if it might feel like that sometimes. Everyone goes through some form of transition as they enter adulthood. And there's support if you'd like it.

Life can feel like a rollercoaster of emotions at times. This could include happiness, motivation, sadness, discouragement, love, excitement, anger, or despair. It's alright, you're going to get through it, and it does get easier.

Some emotions, like joy, excitement, gratitude, and contentment, feel great. And some feel crummy, like loneliness, jealousy, anxiety, or rejection. The negative emotions can be difficult on us, even painful, especially if they're held onto for long periods. My intention is to offer you some support to get through the tough stuff.

Social Media

Social media is a big part of our lives. In this new modern world of tech, just about everyone uses some form of social media, and it's changed the way that we socialize. We can communicate easily with others and build social support systems.

Social media can be used as entertainment and a form of self-expression too! This connection has literally Globalized our World, bringing friends and family together thousands of miles away. It's a very powerful tool!

As incredible as this is, some downsides can be noted, especially for teens. Social media can be distracting and obsessive, disrupt proper sleep, expose teens to bullying, enable the spread of rumors, promote unrealistic views of other people's lives, and influence peer pressure.

Social media, in many ways, has replaced person-to-person confrontation and can be used in nasty ways. It's easier to publicly share mean things about someone, which could embarrass or hurt them when hiding behind a screen or even remaining anonymous.

In addition, this form of *disconnection* through Social Media offers an outlet to say and do things that are harder in person. For example, it may seem like a safe place to share flirty or provocative pictures with love interests.

But the consequences of sexting and sending naked photos online could go viral in a way teens are not prepared for and could be tied to harmful ultimatums like revenge or blackmail.

Lastly, with social media comes the obsession with selfies. No matter how great the selfie is, many teens will measure their worth on how many "likes" or "comments" the picture gets.

This turns the selfie into an addiction and a gauge of their own looks, worth, popularity, and validity.

It's completely normal to feel a wide range of emotions about social media channels. You love them, then despise them, then back again. I get it, and I don't blame you for one second!

Indeed, there are hurdles when it comes to these networks. The most important thing to consider here is balance. Do your best to nurture your self-esteem, good values, in-person contact, and quality time with those you care about. In this way, social media can augment and solidify relationships.

Difficult Emotions

Unfortunately, negative emotions are impossible to avoid, so learning to manage these is where the skill lies. And sometimes, these emotions are overwhelming, like they take over. And it's hard to think about anything else. This is so normal!

You want to develop healthy coping mechanisms to shift these strong negative feelings into positive ones. It takes practice, but if you *notice* your reactions and what you tend to do, you can change them.

Instead of scrolling through social media, binge eating, or isolating yourself, bring awareness into the equation and discover a new way of dealing with those hard emotional times.

The key to developing healthy coping mechanisms is to acknowledge when old habits show up and then commit to new ones. Here are some tactics to support you:

- **Acknowledge:** You don't need to hide from yourself. Suppressing strong emotions can go sideways in many ways. It's perfectly normal to feel strongly about something - try not to judge, shame, or blame yourself for your feelings.

- **Expand your Vocab:** Identify and name your emotions. This is a huge breakthrough in emotional self-management! When you can pinpoint what you feel and why you feel that way, you create solutions that pull you out of the abyss of negativity.

- **Awareness:** Get conscious of any harmful and unhealthy coping strategies you tend toward. When you notice your tendencies, you're able to shift them.

- **Take Action:** Try doing something that makes you happy - even if you don't feel like it! You could write, color, draw, sing, dance, play an instrument, have a bath, organize your closet, read… the list is endless. Take your mind off of what's making you feel terrible. Now I don't mean *ignore* your feelings. You can (and should) revisit them later when you feel clear. But at the time, take steps to consciously shift from a negative to a positive mind frame.

- **Talk it Out:** Try speaking to an adult or trusted friend about how you feel. It's helpful to have someone else understand and care about you. They can also help you navigate tough feelings by having a different perspective.

- **Get Active:** Physical activity helps the brain produce natural chemicals that promote a positive mood. Getting good exercise releases stress and can pull you out of a negative frame of mind.

Bullying

I wish it weren't so, but bullying has been around forever. The way it happens these days has become even more sly, but unfortunately, being bullied is still a thing. There are 6 forms of bullying, and it's possible to experience more than one.

Physical bullying is the most obvious and easiest to identify. This could be kicking, hitting, punching, slapping, shoving, or other physical attacks.

Verbal bullying is when someone uses words, statements, and name-calling to gain power. This could look like insults to belittle, demean, and hurt another person, and it's often done without adults around.

Relational bullies attempt to sabotage another's social standing. These bullies often spread rumors, manipulate situations, and break confidence to increase their own social status.

Cyberbullying is a very significant challenge now. The World is so plugged in, and these bullies can harass their targets anywhere, anytime, without being easily caught. This includes threats, hurtful emails, or text messages through social media... and it can be never-ending for a teen.

Sexual bullying includes harmful and humiliating actions that target a person sexually. This could mean name-calling, crude comments, vulgar gestures, uninvited touching, and sexual proposi-tioning.

Prejudicial bullying is being targeted for being different and encompasses all other bullying. This could be a different race, reli-gion, or sexual orientation.

Each tormentor has a different style and uses different tactics to intimidate their victim. Some kids that bully are sneaky, while others are downright and openly mean.

If you are being bullied or know someone who is, I hope the following will help:

It's Not Your Fault

No one deserves to be treated meanly. Often, a bully treats others as they do to hide their own insecurities. Or this is the only treatment *they* know - and this is how they're treated in their home. Whatever reason they have for being a bully, it's NOT about you or anything you've done to cause this. You don't deserve it. Remember this and be kind to yourself.

Speak Up

If you can find the courage to stand up for yourself, you may find the bully leaves you alone as it's not as easy to harass you. You could say, "That's mean," or "I don't like it when you say that to me." Act confident, even if you don't feel it. Take a deep breath and speak clearly. Maintain eye contact with them and send them the message you won't put up with that kind of meanness.

Record It

Keep a record of all the instances. You'll have proof of their pattern if the bully gets more aggressive. Write down the date, time, location, what was said or done, and who might have heard it. Take screenshots of mean texts and emails.

Report It

Bullying is never OK. Whether you're the victim or you witness others being bullied. Please talk to your teachers, principal, parents, or guardians.

Please be brave and let an appropriate adult know if you're being bullied over social media or anywhere online. If you're afraid your parents will take away your phone or computer, explain that to them.

Protect Yourself

Where possible, walk in groups to ensure your bully hardly gets you alone. Ask people to walk with you between classes. Find safe places at school where you can hang out before, after class, or during breaks. You could join clubs that meet at lunch, in the gym, auditorium, or courtyard - outside the main gathering areas.

Rise Above

Try not to retaliate or be mean back. If you participate in the meanness, you'll likely end up feeling terrible anyhow, and you might give your bully more material to tease you with. Remind yourself that you're doing great, and think of things that make you happy.

Gender Identity

It's common for adolescents to be curious and ask questions about their gender identity during this phase of life. It's an excellent time to search for answers about yourself and who you're attracted to. However, this identity search can be much more intense for some teens and cause a great deal of debilitating distress.

Some teens (from all cultures in all parts of the World) question their gender preferences and feel uncomfortable or disappointed with their assigned gender at birth. They feel the body they were born into doesn't reflect their true self, who they are, or who they identify with. This is considered Gender Dysphoria.

Gender dysphoria describes a sense of unease a person may have due to a mismatch between their biological sex and gender identity. This dissatisfaction can lead to depression and anxiety and could have a harmful impact.

These lines of self-reflection and internal questioning can also lead to peer bullying and discrimination. As well as the fear of being judged by their family members.

For transgender youth going through gender dysphoria, the best thing to do now is to seek support. Talk to your parents first, if you can. If you can't, talk to your school guidance counselor or trusted friends. You can also call a help hotline if you want to remain anonymous while sharing.

Where to Get Help

Even when you're totally overwhelmed with emotion, have no one to talk to, or don't want to share with anyone you know, there are **still** options. Consider reaching out to a help hotline. Most are open 24/7.

You can search for a local number online. There are many resources available for support. Here are a few to get you started.

- **FindaHelpLine.com:** For free emotional support anytime, anywhere.
- **TheHopeLine.com:** A fantastic resource for chat, phone, or email.
- **CheckPointOrg.com/Global:** Lists crisis phone numbers all over the World.
- **HelpGuide.org:** Offers articles and even meditations to support healthy mind frames.
- **UnitedGMH.org:** Supports global mental health in ways.

Please reach out to someone anonymously if you're not comfortable seeking support from someone you know. It's 100% OK to feel awful, ok? Life can be cruel at times. Please know there is help no matter what you're going through. All you need is the courage to reach out.

Kim's Corner: *There's no shame in asking for help.*

I'm not sure where this comes from, but there's a notion that asking for help is a sign of weakness. However, it's actually the opposite! Asking for support when you're not in a good place or if you're struggling, in fact, shows strength, courage, and humility.

Also, asking for help encourages independence, which is ironic if you think about it. It creates room to learn something new if you can admit when you don't know something.

And when you're vulnerable and need help, this is the time to speak to your family and trusted people. You don't have to go through tough stuff alone. If these people care about you, you should never feel any sort of remorse for sharing what's going on.

This is a complicated phase of life, remember. Find a way to get help when you need it - for anything! Asking for help definitely doesn't make you weak. It makes you human!

FIFTEEN

Keys to Wellness

W hat does wellness even mean? It's a positive state of mental health and practicing healthy habits to live a fulfilled life. People who have healthy mental wellness are generally positive. They have a good grasp of their own thoughts, emotions, and behaviors, letting them build solid relationships and enjoy life.

Spirituality

Spirituality has many different meanings with so many cultures, religions, practices, and beliefs on the planet. It can be a deep sense of self-reflection and acceptance. It can also be a belief in a higher entity or being. And it can be the act of beloved daily practices and strong belief systems.

Spirituality is deeply personal, and there's no right or wrong. While the scope of spiritual practice is infinite, there are some simple ways to get started. Here are a few of my favorites:

- **Connect with Nature:** Spending time in nature can increase your spiritual health. You can't help but disconnect from your busy life. Even just a few minutes watching the birds, listening to the wind in the trees, or walking in a field can be therapeutic. It helps add perspective to feel the magnificence and mystery of the world.

- **Breathe:** Our breath is with us everywhere. The more we breathe intentionally, our awareness of our surroundings, environment, others, and our lives are heightened.
- **Meditate:** You don't need to be an expert. It just takes a few minutes a day. Sit quietly, breathe slowly, and empty your mind of problems and rapid thinking. Imagine clouds slowly drifting, and then focus on your breath. When you drift into thoughts, gently remind yourself of the clouds again. You don't even have to sit. Try a *walking* meditation. Be mindful of your steps and feet on the ground. You can do this anywhere, anytime. Just slow your mind down and become present.
- **Connect with Community:** Reach out to a Spiritual or Religious Leader and find ways to be with like-minded people within your community who can support and encourage you. Find people that share your beliefs and thoughts and connect with them.
- **Create a Practice:** Make a routine out of a process that includes faith, hope, and love. This may be lighting candles on Friday nights, reciting a short personal prayer each night before sleep, or it could be a grace before meals, or writing in your Gratitude journal each day. Whatever you do, commit to the practice that lets you focus on hope and trust.
- **Journal:** The act of physically writing helps process emotions, increase awareness, and provides a nonjudgmental space of expression. Turn the process into a positive practice by focusing on gratitude. Jot down things that make you feel good, and keep your focus on the expectation that good things will come to you.

Self-Esteem

For me, fully loving yourself consists of a few related but different parts; self-esteem, self-worth, and self-compassion. I'll briefly cover these in the following sections.

Self-esteem is the opinion we have of ourselves. With healthy self-esteem, we feel positive about ourselves and life in general. We can easily manage life's ups and downs and handle challenges that arise.

Low self-esteem often begins in childhood. When we're young, we often attach a negative meaning to a situation because we don't fully *understand* the complete scenario. For example, we didn't get chosen in the 'Red Rover' game and made this mean we weren't good enough. Or our parents got divorced, and we made it mean we're not loveable.

We created a negative meaning out of something we didn't understand- because we were kids! And these experiences can add up throughout life, adding evidence to an already skewed belief about ourselves. A typical message becomes "I'm not good enough" or "it's all my fault." You get the point...

Here are some activities you can do to combat these false beliefs.

- **Write a List:** Compile a list of things you love about yourself. What do you appreciate and admire?
- **Don't People Please:** People with low self-esteem often put others before themselves. It's nice to be helpful, but your self-esteem will wear thin if you tie your value to how much you do for others.
- **Stop Comparing:** This can be tricky in a digital world where people put the best, most flattering parts of their life online for display. Balancing exposure to social media will help. And remember, we're all unique little humans with talents in many different areas. If you're comparing

yourself to others, you're forgetting to appreciate what YOU'RE great at. Try and focus your efforts there.

- **Be Kind:** Be gentle to yourself when you're feeling self-critical. Consider what you might say to someone you care about in a similar situation. We often give better advice to others than we take for ourselves.

- **Celebrate:** Be proud of yourself for your achievements! Maybe you hit a goal? Did you push past fear or negative belief? Or perhaps you simply got up and got dressed without tumbling into depression. Wherever you are, there's room for celebration. Focus on what's going well and acknowledge the victories, no matter how small they seem.

- **Self Talk:** What are the messages you're telling yourself? Are you too hard on yourself? As a test, write down some of the things you say to yourself for a week. If these are not things you'd say to a good friend, rewrite them kindly and refer to them when you fall back into old sayings.

Self-esteem is what we think, feel, and believe about ourselves, and can shift from moment to moment and day to day.

Self-Worth

Self-worth is the internal belief of being valuable and worthy of love, just as you are.

Rather than relying on external factors such as successes and achievements, self-worth is more about the *foundations* of loving yourself. It's about giving yourself the same respect, dignity, care, and understanding you want for the people you love.

Having low self-worth can let depression set in, permit risky behaviors, tolerate abusive treatment, and allow feelings of failure to detain you from reaching your potential.

Although this is foundational, there definitely are ways you can improve your self-worth. Still, it takes consistent work to adopt new intrinsic beliefs about ourselves. It starts by shifting habitual thoughts from negative to positive ones.

The following are sayings individuals with a high sense of self-worth will say or think to themselves. Try adopting these sayings. It'll pay off in virtually all areas of your life.

"No matter what, I'm worthy of love."

Accept your mistakes but don't shame yourself. Separate what occurred from WHO you are. Say, "I made a bad choice," rather than "I'm a bad person." Own mistakes where you need to, and make them right. Nobody's perfect, and you're not bad in any way!

"It's OK to feel what I'm feeling."

Create space for your emotions without feeling guilty. Emotions are our internal guide, so it's great to pay attention to them. Feelings are never *wrong*, no matter what the feeling is. Notice your emotions, and let them be. When you're done feeling it, let it go.

"It's not about what *happened*; it's how I *respond* to it."

Life can get tricky, no doubt. The magic is in how we *choose* to react to situations. Rather than getting stuck in the emotions of what's happened, a more powerful approach is to move forward with whatever new information was gathered.

"I find things to be grateful for."

If you implement only ONE thing from this book, I hope it's this. Gratitude, particularly a daily practice of gratitude, is your ticket to a richer, happier life. Find ways to appreciate the big and small gifts of life. It's easy to be grateful when things are going well. The challenge is to notice something to be thankful for when things are not going well. This takes practice. And you'll develop this muscle over time but keep at it. The payoff is life-long.

"I love who I am inside and out."

Fundamentally, this is the key to high self-worth. Get curious about why you're not feeling good about who you are. Acceptance is the first part, and then let go of what you can't change. Acknowledge, embrace, and celebrate the wonderful things about yourself.

"I am in charge of my life."

You have the power to change things in your life when things aren't going well. You can pursue any dream and accomplish anything you put your mind and muscle into with determination, persistence, and a good plan - the World is yours!

Self-worth is our belief system. And we need to nurture this with self-compassion. Can you see how these are all related?

Self-Compassion

For me, this is a critical part of fully loving ourselves. For some, it might be simple, while others need to work at it. But it's worth it.

Self-compassion is the ability to turn understanding, acceptance, and love inward. It's when we can bring kindness and understanding to our mistakes rather than self-criticism and feeling inadequate.

When we're compassionate with ourselves, we experience support and encouragement in the face of adversity. And with an inner knowledge that struggles and challenges are a part of life and everyone goes through them.

This is about being kind to yourself, even when things don't happen as expected. And acknowledging it's OK to be imperfect. So how can you cultivate this?

- **Common Grounds:** I promise you're not alone in whatever you feel. Many teens realize that what they're feeling, whether it's fear, insecurity, depression, exclusion, etc., is common among their peers. It might not always seem that way, but everyone at this phase of life is going through *something*. Life isn't fair, but it isn't fair for everyone, which makes it more fair!

- **Practice Mindfulness:** When you feel like you can't manage all the emotions inside, slow down your mind and focus on your feet, your breath, or what you can hear at that moment. Mindfulness is paying attention to and keeping your focus on something intentionally.

- **Forgive Yourself:** It's OK to make mistakes. In fact, it's an integral part of life. Go easy on yourself and remember you're human. Perfection is a facade. There's always room for improvement on all levels. Be proud of yourself for what you've done, how far you've come, and progress you've made. Forgive yourself for being imperfect.

- **Supportive Self-Talk:** Notice the conversations which take place within your mind. Are your inner voices critical or loving? If they're the former, the first step is to acknowledge, then you can actively shift your thoughts to include self-compassion. Call in your 'inner cheerleader' voice, which supports you through difficult times.

Happiness & Staying Positive

We've talked a lot about different ways to shift your thinking from negative to positive. I won't repeat myself here, but want to include these final tips:

- **Get to Know You:** Pay attention to what you're feeling and what you *need* to feel happy. Expressing this through a journal is an excellent way of understanding yourself.

- **Be Social:** Make time for family and friends - share the ups and downs, so you don't keep things inside.

- **Be Conscious:** It takes practice, but if you can notice when you're not feeling happy, this is the first step to shifting it. When you add consciousness to how you feel, you have a choice. You can decide to take steps to feel better - or not. But it IS a choice. I realize there will be times when it's appropriate not to feel good. I'm not saying you should pretend to be happy. I'm saying when you're ready, and if you choose to, you can consciously turn things around.

- **Gratitude:** Focus on one thing you can be grateful for. Start there. Even if it's just being thankful that it's sunny outside or that you live close enough to the ocean, you can walk to the shore and listen to the waves. Anything. It's impossible to be genuinely grateful and be negative at the same time. Try it!

- **Laugh:** It's true; laughter really is the best medicine. It takes more muscles to frown than it does to smile! Also, it's tough to be sad when you smile. Next time you feel down, head into the bathroom and smile at yourself for 30 seconds. I promise it will change how you feel!

- **Trust:** At the risk of sounding cliche, when one door closes, another opens. There are opportunities literally everywhere! If you've been turned down a road you didn't expect, do your best to trust that things will work out just as they were meant to.

- **Let It Go:** In life, things are going to happen you're not super happy about. Put on invisible armor and let bad feelings bounce off you. It's OK to feel it, but don't dwell and feel sorry for yourself. Take the lesson, and discard the rest!

- **Give Back:** An intrinsic sense of joy bubbles up when you give back. Find ways to regularly give to others. It doesn't always have to be a charity. You could visit your grandmother, buy a coffee for a friend or offer a sandwich to a homeless person. All kind acts count!

Kim's Corner: *You have a CHOICE to be Happy!!*

Albeit somewhat challenging to hear and accept at times, **there is always a choice to be positive** and, ultimately, to be happy.

I didn't say it was always an easy choice!

When we're feeling emotions that lower our energetic vibration, like fear, sadness, loneliness, anger, jealousy, insecurity, guilt, or shame - often, there's an *attachment* to feeling this way. This attachment can be unconscious, but there's something in it for us to hold onto the negative feeling.

Think about a negative emotion you regularly feel and WHY you're holding onto it. What do you get out of feeling upset or disappointed? Please write it down so it becomes easier to process.

Next, look at what you wrote, and consider one or two positive aspects you could focus on instead. If this is challenging, try talking out loud as if you're talking TO someone. Sometimes, this opens us up to receive ideas.

For example, your younger brother ripped apart your closet, and your clothes and shoes are everywhere! Apart from the mess you now have to clean up, you could go through and repack your dresser better. Or maybe it's a perfect opportunity to go through your clothes and donate what you don't wear.

My point is that there's always another way of looking at everything. Glass half full instead of half empty, right? You have a choice when it comes to your personal attitude, even if that choice is a difficult one to make some days! When you take personal responsibility for how you feel, even in the face of adversity and challenges, you set yourself up for success, and you'll go far.

Conclusion

Well done! You've made it so far already, and you'll undoubtedly go even further. As you venture out into newfound independence, remember **life is a journey**, a dance of learning filled with lessons and losses, beautiful wonders, excitement, anticipation, and glory!

The life skills you begin learning during your teens will continue to develop as you get older. Learning never stops, even into your senior years! Keep your mind open to continuous growth, and you will succeed as a happy, healthy, and prosperous individual.

I sincerely hope this book has offered you valuable life-skills knowledge. As well as insight into the many areas of life you'll explore; physically, mentally, socially, and emotionally. Thank you for trusting me with your precious time and resources.

If you enjoyed reading this book, please leave a positive review, so others can be supported through this time of life.

Finally, I'd like to leave you with a quote from Charlie Wardle, which I love.

"A bird sitting on a tree branch is never afraid of the branch breaking because its trust is not on the branch, but on its own wings."

You are perfect, just as you are.

Trust yourself; you were born to fly.

And always believe in yourself.

Sending you much love,

Kim xo

77925646R00094